Daniel Lee

Taxpayers of Norwich

Political hand book

Daniel Lee

Taxpayers of Norwich
Political hand book

ISBN/EAN: 9783337134105

Printed in Europe, USA, Canada, Australia, Japan

Cover: Foto ©Suzi / pixelio.de

More available books at **www.hansebooks.com**

AND

POLITICAL HAND BOOK

COMPILED BY

DANIEL LEE.

1884.

PRINTED BY THE DAY COMPANY, NEW LONDON, CONN.

In presenting this book to the public, I desire to return thanks to those whose generous patronage of its advertising pages has made its publication possible. It contains the announcements of many of the leading manufacturers and merchants of this city. The scope and purpose of the work need no explanation. It is believed that it will prove valuable as a work of reference on many points. The political statistics will be found useful and interesting in a presidential year. I cannot hope that the volume will be entirely free from errors, but it has been prepared with care and, it is believed, will be found correct in every material point. Should a favorable reception be accorded this venture it is my intention to continue the publication, with such changes and additions as experience may suggest, annually hereafter. THE COMPILER.

CONTENTS.

INDEX TO ADVERTISERS.

HINTS TO PROPERTY OWNERS.

The most important thing for every person owning property is to hand in a list of all, whether real or personal, to the Assessors during the month of October in each year, which must be sworn to. If this duty is neglected, the Assessors are instructed to make out a list of such property as they have reason to believe is owned by any such person and liable to taxation, and add 10 per cent. of such valuation. If neglected the following year 20 per cent. shall be added. The third year 30 per cent., and so on.

The Assessors meet between October 15th, and set daily until November 1st. The Board of Relief meet on the first Monday in January and sit twenty days thereafter to listen to appeals from the doings of the Assessors. The Board have power to reduce or increase the list of any person under certain conditions. Every person in possession of property on the first day of October liable to taxation must hand in the list. Upon this list the Town tax is laid and made payable on the 20th of February following. The city tax is laid on same list and made payable on the 1st of October following. Although nearly a year intervenes between the time of handing in the lists and the time the city tax is payable, the person who lists the property is liable for the city tax. In other words the city tax follows the person, and not the property. School taxes, however, follows the property and not the person, consequently the purchaser of a parcel of real estate before the School tax is laid is liable for the tax. The town tax is laid at the annual town meeting, held on the first Monday in October, and payable February 20th, following. The City tax is laid at the annual city meeting the 1st Monday in June and payable October 1st, following. The School tax in the Central District is laid in July and payable October 1st, following. In the Greeneville District, the tax is payable in April. West Chelsea District in May, and the Falls District in June.

Every person between the ages of 21 and 70 years shall pay a poll tax of one dollar and no more for town and state purposes. Those paying a commutation or military tax are not liable to pay a poll tax. One hundred dollars is added to every man's school list who pays a poll tax. Those purchasing real estate cannot be too careful in looking after back taxes. See the tax collector and inquire if the taxes are all paid before taking a deed of the property. This course saves trouble and expense.

The following are the names of those who pay taxes in the Town of Norwich with the amounts for which they are assessed. It also includes the non-resident taxpayers, pension exempts and exempt property:

Name	Amount
Abner, Randall J.	$500
Aborn, Alonzo R.	9,250
Adams, Paulina J.	1,400
Adams, Daniel T.	1,300
Adams, John T., est of	15,750
Adams & Reynolds,	2,300
Ahern, Thomas	1,600
Aiken, William A.	28,659
Albro, Francis D.	1,430
Alexander, Charles H.	1,200
Alexander, Phebe M., est	2,200
Allan, James	7,450
Allen, Amos D.	40
Allen, Charles H.	4,825
Allen, Edwin	3,165
Allen, Henry	24,900
Allen, Henry & Son	2,700
Allen, James	120
Allen, J. Arthur	60
Allen, Nelson R.	150
Allen Spool Printing Co.	5,000
Allyn, Calvin	6,365
Alleman, John	1,000
Almy, Albert H.	60
Almy, Leonard B.	200
Anderson, George	330
Andrews, P. St. M.	5,200
Anthony, Joseph	1,140
Appleton, Henry P.	2,175
Armstrong, Horace W.	1,300
Armstrong, William A.	150
Armstrong, Lorenzo D.	2,890
Armstrong, William H.	475
Arnold & Hiscox	1,800
Arnold, James H.	2,325
Arnold, Mary O.	900
Arnold, Sylvester	2,360
Atchison, Robert, est	984
Atchison, Walter T.	700
Austin, Willis R.	50,650
Averill, John C.	50
Avery, Charles G.	2,200
Avery, Charles S.	3,550
Avery, Henrietta L., est	800
Avery, H. D.	775
Avery, Olive R., est	500
Avery, Oliver P.	9,050
Avery, William W.	11,050

Name	Amount
Ayer, Delia M.	$690
Ayer, Elisha	9,800
Bachelder, Jacob B.	2,500
Backus, Asa	26,125
Backus, Asa & est. S. B. Case	10,000
Backus, Cynthia M.	11,800
Backus, James, est	5,200
Backus, Mrs. Mary F.	1,000
Backus, William W	1,283
Bacon Arms Co.	20,000
Bacon, Leonard W.	22,191
Bailey, Albert A.	3,330
Bailey, Charles H.	110
Bailey, Mrs. Emily M.	200
Bailey, Mrs. Mary A	1,650
Bailey, Otis G.	6,350
Bailey, Sarah	2,450
Bailey, Youngs A.	275
Baird, James W.	510
Baker, James, est	2,700
Balcom, Edward F.	425
Baldwin, Charles B.	10,300
Baldwin, Charles L.	400
Baldwin, Elisha B.	3,300
Baldwin, Jabez B.	8,300
Baldwin, Jedediah	850
Balfour, Robert	14,453
Ballou, Leonard B., est	33,340
Banning, J. Q.	220
Barber, J. E. & Co.	1,000
Barber, Rowland B.	6,537
Barber, Thurston B.	3,310
Bard, Charles	14,240
Bard & Dorrance & Gibbs	4,000
Bard, George F.	2,910
Barlow, Mrs Henry	800
Barnes & Company	7,000
Barnes, Emeline, est	3,500
Barney, Benjamin J.	225
Barney, Thomas J., est	120
Barrows, Edwin S.	4,712
Barrows, Henry A.	3,800
Barry, Bridget S.	425
Barry, Maurice	800
Barry, Michael	3,010
Barry, Mrs. Winnifred	1,600

Name	Amount
Barstow, John P.	$16,775
Barstow, John P. & Co.	8,175
Bartlett, R. S.	1,675
Bassett, Susan A.	400
Battin & Taylor,	6,000
Batty, Mrs. Emma G.	1,250
Baum, Samuel	800
Bauman, Edward N.	400
Bauman, Nicholas	800
Beach, William L.	2,100
Beaumont, Nathaniel	720
Beckwith, Ansel A.	4,650
Beckwith, Charles	1,155
Beckwith, Elias H	11,475
Beckwith, Eliphalet	3,750
Beckwith, Elisha W.	2,430
Beckwith, Emily H	231
Beckwith, Frank E	1,200
Beckwith, Lester T., est.	700
Beckwith & Setchell,	5,500
Beebe, Alfred R.	1,665
Beebe, Alfred S., est.	2,900
Beebe, Charles H	550
Beebe, Mrs. Daniel F	630
Beebe, Joab F., est.	1,250
Beebe, Sarah A.	1,415
Beers, Oliver T.	1,560
Begley, John	125
Behrisch, Bernard.	3,550
Belknap, Frank S.	700
Ball, Jackson	920
Bellefleuer, Magloire	880
Benjamin, Daniel W	3,820
Benjamin, George H.	590
Benjamin, Jacob C	1,700
Benshadler, Caspar	375
Benson, John R.	900
Bent, Martin F.	2,325
Bentley, David N., trustee	1,400
Bentley, Fanny B.	700
Bentley, Lorenzo D.	11,950
Bentley, Mrs. Mary	200
Berry, Gorton	3,300
Bestor, C. Jane	2,000
Bestor, George R.	10,051
Beswick, John	1,200
Bidwell, Charles T.	$2,570
Bidwell, E. George	3,495
Bidwell, Mrs. Eliza G.	1,500
Bidwell, Francis A.	2,650
Bidwell, Halsey F.	3,500
Bidwell, Bachelder & Co.	3,000
Bill, Elijah A.	1,325
Bill, Henry	95,290
Bill, Henry, trustee	1,500
Bill, Henry & Gurdon	45,000
Bill, Henry Publishing Co.	31,500
Bill, Palmer	1,700
Bill & Durfey	1,200
Billings, David A.	1,050
Bills, George C	7,550
Bingham, Nathan A.	11,475
Birchard, Justin W.	1,375
Birkery, James.	125
Birkery, Thomas.	900
Birraeree, John	1,200
Birraeree, Michael	2,000
Bishop, George G	2,725
Bishop, Herbert M.	5,875
Bishop, Nathan L.	4,300
Bishop, Sherman B.	2,050
Bisket & Meech,	1,125
Blackburn, John	1,000
Blackman, Lucy A. W.	3,000
Blake, John E	2,150
Blackstone, J. DeT.	8,525
Blackstone, Mrs. J. DeT	1,700
Blackstone, Lorenzo	38,130
Bliss, Alvan B	1,200
Bliss, Charles C.	16,825
Bliss, Lydia L.	12,000
Bliss, Willard, est	3,000
Bliss, William H.	2,175
Bliven, Samuel B.	325
Boardman, Byron	7,320
Boardman, Clement, est	720
Boardman, James	3,185
Boehler, Herman	1,025
Bogue, Israel	1,175
Bothwick, Alexander C.	4,350
Boston & Norwich Clothing Co.	3,500
Boswell, John L.	3,675
Boswell, Mary G.	1,800

Bottom, George G. $2,525
Bottom, William D. 1,500
Bottomley, Joseph A 1,000
Bower, Mrs. Maria H 2,880
Bowers, Gilbert 75
Bowler, Michael 1,200
Bowman, John R 3,300
Bouchard, Victor 1,340
Boyle, John 500
Bradbury, James 2,485
Brady, Charles E. 1,900
Brambach, Daniel L. 200
Branch, Mrs. E. B. 1,200
Branch, Walter H. 500
Brand, Minnie H 1,800
Brand, Temperance A 4,100
Braun, Lorenzo 2,040
Bray, Joseph 330
Brayton, Samuel L. 1,400
Brakenridge, Robert, ...1,200
Breed, Benjamin F., est 1,800
Breed, Edward. 2,000
Breed, John, est. 45,000
Brennan, Humphrey 1,250
Brennan, James, 1st. 1,240
Brewer, Abby M. 10,450
Brewer, Arthur R. 3,000
Brewer, Edward P. 220
Brewer, Harriet T., est 6,000
Brewer, John M. 4,500
Brewer, Pliny 10,580
Brewer, William L. 5,600
Brewer, William L., trustee. 2,645
Brewster, Benjamin F 3,450
Brewster Brothers, ...875
Brewster, Elias M. 3,000
Brewster, John D 3,065
Brewster, Walter S. 2,550
Brewster & Barnett 4,300
Briggs, Charles E. 1,800
Briggs, Horace A 6,370
Briggs, William 2,000
Briscoe, Willis A. 200
Broadway Cong'l Society, ...2,000
Brock, Thomas $150
Bromley, Charles P. 1,575
Bromley, Mrs. James B. 5,200
Brooks, George E. 1,200
Broun, Castilla B. 1,300
Brown, Bartholomew 1,400
Brown, Charles H 670
Brown, Daniel 330
Brown, Daniel J. 1,600
Brown, Francis G 1,700
Brown, Franklin H. 2,000
Brown, George E. 1,590
Brown, Governor H 2,950
Brown, Harriet K 3,510
Brown, Henry N 1,510
Brown, James A. 7,250
Brown, Jonathan M. 192
Brown, Lucius 4,250
Brown, Mary A. 1,600
Brown, Mrs. Nancy M 2,300
Brown, Patrick 1,300
Brown, Patrick, 2d. 352
Brown, Reuben B. 1,700
Brown, Robert 9,650
Brown, Theron E 525
Brown, William R. 1,100
Brown, William T. 1,000
Brown, Lucius, assignee. 11,502
Browning, Amos A. 18
Browning, Charles D 10,800
Browning, C. D. & Co. 12,200
Browning, John 2,719
Bruce, George H. 225
Bruce & Baird, ...800
Brush, De Witt 115
Brushell, Mary Esther 330
Buckingham, Lydia A. 34,125
Buckingham, William A 3,825
Buckley, Elizabeth. 550
Buckley, Michael 900
Buckley, Timothy 500
Buckley, William 1,369
Bulkeley, Helen M. W. 11,115
Bulkeley, Samuel B 7,100

Bulletin Association, ... $29,000
Bulletin Company, ... 12,000
Burdick, Evan, est 12,500
Burke, Bridget 2,500
Burke, Charles F. 1,900
Burke, Frank 1,200
Burke, James 570
Burke, Sarah 900
Burke, William. 3,100
Burnham, Charles A., est 5,200
Burnham, W. R. 1,650
Burns, Edward 1,400
Burns, Martin 1,276
Burns, Mrs. Mary 440
Burns, Michael 600
Burns, Roger 1,275
Burns, Philip 700
Burr, Walter 1,200
Burton, Thomas 3,300
Burton, William 5,250
Burton, William, 2d 225
Bushnell, Charles P. 375
Bushnell, Chauncey K 8,075
Bushnell, George T. 2,175
Bushnell, Jabez W. 1,570
Bushnell, James E. 1,040
Bushnell, James F. 2,585
Bushnell, Martin, est 584
Bushnell, Richard T. 900
Bushnell, William H. 7,755
Butler, Mrs. James 2,855
Butler, John 1,140
Butler, Sarah A 400
Butterfield, James A 3,150
Button, Abby S. 1,500
Button, John A. 220
Button, Lucius L 2,530
Button, Samuel A. 700
Byles, George S. 250
Byrnes, Joseph 1,020

Callahan, John 700
Callahan, Patrick 900

Camp, Frederick S. $6,825
Caoghlin, William 400
Capen, Philip A. 1,300
Capron, Clarence P. 3,450
Cardwell, William H. 5,610
Cardwell & Wait, ... 4,100
Carew, Charles J. 450
Carew, Henry W. 995
Carew, James S., est. 23,336
Carew, Mrs Jennie A. 8,000
Carew, Mary A. 200
Carey, Andrew E. 4,050
Carey, Charles W. 2,800
Carey, Frederick W. 12,800
Carey, James 1,520
Carleton, Charles M 5,550
Carpenter, Delano N. 350
Carpenter, Gerard, est, ... 2,200
Carpenter, Harriet L 630
Carpenter, Increase W. 12,000
Carpenter, Joseph H. 3,145
Carrier, Joseph B 1,625
Carrier, Titus 1,000
Carroll, Adams P 240
Carroll, Frank 1,200
Carroll, Joseph 1,225
Carroll, Lucius W 37,490
Carroll, L. W., & Son, ... 10,000
Carswell, James 1,000
Caruthers, William 550
Carter, Joseph 3,150
Carter, Samuel, est 8,900
Case, Elizabeth 1,800
Case, George, est. 1,700
Case, Fanny M. 3,400
Case, Jennie A. 2,000
Case, Louise M. 1,115
Case, Luther R. 5,725
Case, Samuel 9,650
Case, William T. 575
Case & Fuller, ... 10,150
Casey, Michael, 1st, ... 900
Casey, Michael, 2d, ... 120
Casey, Patrick 390

Casey, Thomas	$400
Casey, William, est	700
Cash, Imogene A.	1,500
Cassidy, Patrick M. D.	11,650
Cassidy, Patrick	900
Caswell, Anna, est.	1,200
Cauley, Rosa	240
Caulkins, John H.	1,000
Caulkins, Nancy	1,680
Chace, Benjamin C.	2,345
Chaffee, Josiah H	120
Chamansky, Joseph	1,800
Chamberlain, C. E. P.	7,000
Chamberlain, George G.	2,000
Champlin, Charles N.	6,215
Champlin, Henry	1,300
Champlin, Francis I	3,200
Champlin, William G.	2,500
Chandler, Charles E.	1,675
Chapdelaine, Joseph	3,350
Chapdelaine, Pierre	2,100
Chapman, Amos	2,000
Chapman, Byron S.	350
Chapman, Charles B.	2,650
Chapman, Enoch F.	5,900
Chapman, Fanny H	2,000
Chapman, Festus	820
Chapman, Harvey	6,100
Chapman, Nathaniel and Harvey	2,500
Chapman, Mary A., est	3,000
Chapman, Mrs. Mary A.	25,525
Chapman, Nathan L.	900
Chapman, Mrs. Hariet H	4,800
Chapman, Sanford A.	8,200
Chapman, Stephen O.	720
Chapman & Rist,	3,175
Chapel, Caroline R.	3,680
Chappell, Charles W.	4,445
Chappell, Edward	92,845
Chappell, Edward, & Co.	31,700
Charlton, Mary S	800
Chase, Mary A., est	2,200
Chase, Stephen S.	800
Chelsea File Works,	1,000
Chelsea Paper Manufacturing Co.	$297,150
Chelsea Savings Bank,	15,000
Cheney, Harriet C.	1,100
Cherry, Andrew	1,500
Cherry, George	1,200
Cherry, James	1,800
Cheesbrough, Catherine	360
Cheesbrough, Nancy D.	8,700
Childs, Alfred S.	350
Christ Church Parish	3,000
Church, Fanny C.	1,200
Church, Roxana	360
Church, William L.	93
Clapp, Edward T	3,650
Clapp, Mrs. Martha	1,650
Clapp, Wales W.	90
Clark, Albert A	800
Clark, Alfred L.	6,500
Clark, Ansel	14,565
Clark, Chester	50
Clark, David P.	1,120
Clark, Edwin D.	5,500
Clark, George L.	2,700
Clark, George R.	7,420
Clark, James N.	8,825
Clark, John T.	3,350
Clark, Mrs. Sarah J.	2,400
Clark, Willis W.	1,800
Clark, Jeannett	80
Clifford, Andrew	600
Clifford, Daniel	2,025
Clifford, Michael	370
Clifford, Michael, 2d,	1,212
Clinton Mills Company	115,250
Clune, Patrick	330
Cobb, Amos E.	14,916
Cobb, Charles H.	1,500
Cobb, Lloyd M	100
Cochrane, Almira N.	600
Coffee, Eugene, est	600
Coffee, James S.	2,050
Coffee, John	1,469
Cogswell, Charles P.	19,250
Coit, Charles M., heirs	8,000

Coit, George D.	$8,250
Coit, Harriet C.	2,575
Coit, Mary B.	6,300
Coit, Nancy M., est.	9,000
Colbert, Daniel	700
Colburn, Richard	7,675
Cole, Mowry B.	2,100
Cole, Otis F., Mrs.	600
Cole, Samuel A.	2,125
Collins, Henry, heirs	2,000
Collins, James P., & Co.	10,800
Collins, Michael	700
Colton, Mary H.	7,775
Colyer, Christopher, est.	2,000
Colyer, Mrs. Michael	3,200
Combra, Frederick	600
Comstock, Albert S	200
Comstock, Samuel	75
Comstock, Thomas	1,800
Conant, Jerome F.	120
Congdon, David, est.	9,900
Congdon, Gilbert L.	5,400
Congdon, Joel	750
Congdon, Patrick R.	5,250
Congdon, William H.	1,100
Conlan, Michael E.	600
Connell, Ellen	1,020
Connell, Mary	550
Connell, Michael	100
Connell, Michael, 2d	110
Connelly, Dennis	1,300
Connelly, John	550
Connors & Barry	2,400
Connors, Jeremiah	487
Connors & Rigney	275
Connors, James	80
Connor, Joseph	5,125
Connor, Patrick	480
Connor, T. J. & Co.	580
Conrade, John	800
Converse, Albert T.	18,975
Converse, Charles A.	37,292
Converse, Mrs. F. D. T	15,600
Conway, James	600
Cook, Mrs. Abby A.	11,500
Cook, Mrs. Abby C.	$575
Cook, Adin	9,125
Cook, Charles G.,	1,000
Cook, Edward T.	4,500
Cook, Henry L.	7,500
Cook, Hiram	3,300
Cook, Nathan	110
Cook, Mrs. Sarah L.	150
Cook, William A.	10,900
Cook, W. Avery	145
Coombs, Emeline M	2,200
Coon, Amos	600
Coon, Denison P.	16,650
Coon & Lucas	2,500
Cooney, Michael, est.	600
Cooper, Peter	1,700
Copp, William H.	2,310
Corcoran, Stephen	80
Corey, Elias R.	3,066
Corkery, Mrs. Margaret	1,825
Corkery, John	3,800
Cosgrove, James F. & Co.	2,650
Cottrell, Elias	2,900
Coughlin, Catherine	2,800
Coughlin, David A.	687
Coughlin, Jeremiah	1,000
Coughlin, Mary	1,100
Coughlin, William	1,100
Connihan, Daniel	1,700
Connihan, Francis	1,200
Courtney, James	1,800
Courtney, Mary	1,000
Cowan, William R.	1,525
Coyle, John	4,000
Crandall, Mrs. Frances E.	4,300
Crane, Mrs. Sarah L.	2,600
Crane, Stephen	2,600
Cranston, Benjamin T.	2,600
Cranston, George E.	1,200
Cranston, John H	16,725
Cramer, William	675
Crary, John W.	2,040
Crawley, Alvah, est	3,200
Crawley, Mrs. Emeline	1,000
Creighton, Mary	1,800
Crocker, Mrs. Abby	360
Crocker, George C.	1,000
Crompton, Thomas	825

Cronin, James W.	$800
Crosby, Mrs. Nancy E.	3,000
Crosby, Hiram, est.	1,150
Crosgrove, Thomas	700
Cross, Isham	3,007
Cross, Royal B.	1,250
Crowell, Zadoc C.	9,675
Crowell, Lewis & Co.	4,000
Cruthers, James	1,290
Cruttenden, Henry B.	1,700
Cryer, George	5,250
Cryer, George R.	2,575
Cummings Daniel	2,750
Cummings, Patrick	2,000
Cummings, Thomas	240
Cunningham, John H	2,850
Cunningham, Thomas	10,050
Cunningham, William F	150
Currier Brothers	2,000
Currier, Jacob M.	75
Currier, Richard H.	2,650
Cutler, Louise G	900
Curtis, Alfred E.	3,300
Curtis, Laura J.	1,000
Dale, William	900
Daley, John est	3,200
Daley, Mrs. Maurice	1,680
Daley, William	950
Davis, Alpha E.	2,225
Davis, Alonzo B	302
Davis, Alvan T.	300
Davis, Charles H.	5,600
Davis, Charles H., 2nd	125
Davis, Fanny	1,650
Davis, Francis	4,000
Davis, George W.	1,800
Davis, Jeremiah	3,023
Davis & Kinne	12,125
Davison, William H	800
Dawson, James, Jr	1,835
Dawson, Thomas B.	4,655
Day, Ellen	700
Day, Norman	14,975
Dean, Anson F.	1,350
Dean, Edmund W.	1,300
Dearing, Henry	220
Dearing, Mrs. James	$400
Delaney, Michael	1,500
Dempsey, Nicholas	3,060
Deneff, John	2,300
Denison, George W.	1,375
Dennis, Mrs. Cornelia C.	600
Desmond, Eliza	520
Desmond, John	2,000
Desmond, Timothy	600
Devine, John	400
Devine, Nancy	420
Dewey, George L.	115
Dewire, Michael	600
DeWolf, Miss E.	300
Dexter, Albert H.	1,350
Dexter, Merritt D.	2,225
Dickey, A. W. & Co.	4,850
Dickinson, D. M. & Co	13,440
Dime Savings Bank	10,000
Dillaby, Charles H.	2,375
Dimmock, Orrin C.	3,000
Dixon, James	1,300
Dodd, John	6,500
Dodd, Thomas	1,300
Dodge, Samuel R	805
Dolbeare, Christopher R.	300
Dolbeare, Mary G.	2,425
Donahue, Julia	600
Donnelly, Catherine	120
Donnelly, Patrick	522
Donnelly, Patrick, Jr.	1,300
Donavan Daniel	2,000
Donavan, John	900
Donavan, Julia	200
Donavan, Mrs. Patrick	3,000
Doolittle, Dwight	5,700
Doolittle, Mary F.	2,700
Douglass, Leland	1,134
Dowdall, Daniel	1,020
Dowdall, Daniel, Jr	700
Dowd Horace, est	1,600
Dowe, Francis E.	5,700
Dowling, Mrs. M.	990
Doyle, Mary	1,500
Doyle, Nicholas	1,200
Draper, Francis T.	1,400
Driscoll, Dennis	700
Driscoll, Dennis & Patrick	1,500

Drohan, John E	$700
Drummond. Thomas	2,190
Drysdale, Robert	1,155
Dudley, Lucins	4,800
Duggan, James	2,050
Dunn, Bernard	1,500
Durfey, Frank B	14,810
Durfey, Mrs. Harmony	6,650
Durfey, Henry M.	4,590
Durr, George	1,050
Durr, John	1,615
Durr, Martin	225
Durgan, James O.	510
Dyer, Mrs. Abigail C.	65
Dyer, Charles E	25
Dyer, Elijah, est	5,500
Eaglesham, George	2,225
Earl, Fanny M., in trust	2,200
Earnshaw, John	850
Eaton, Mrs. Giles M.	3,200
Eaton, Mrs. Lydia K.	3,000
Eaton, Ruth A	2,200
Eaton & Bailey	375
Eccleston, Harriet M.	550
Edgerton, George H., est.	700
Edgerton, Henry	600
Edmiston, Joseph	1,000
Edmond, Henry V.	5,995
Edmond, J. A.	25
Edmond, Mary H	100
Eggleston, Emeline S	16,335
Eldridge, Theodore H	3,525
Elkey, Harvey E.	600
Ellal, John	600
Elliott, Mrs. Mary J	2,500
Ely, Edwin S.	11,900
Ely, William G.	17,300
Emmons, Alexander H.	4,203
Engler, Andrew	250
English, Mrs. Mary	950
Enos, Frank, Jr.	160
Enos, Frank	797
Enright, James	1,500
Enright, John	5,460
Enright, John, 2d	2,600
Evarts, Daniel R	1,650
Fagan, Sylvester	$30
Fahey, Mary	300
Fahey, John	60
Falls Company	382,150
Fanning, George W.	1,500
Fargo, Mrs. Henry	1,000
Farnsworth, C. Billings.	8,380
Farnsworth, Mrs. Harriet B.	6,150
Farrell, James	1,650
Farrell, James W.	1,400
Farrell, Patrick	980
Farrell, Thomas	80
Farrell, William	275
Farrington, Mrs. Esther H	2,000
Farrington, William T.	100
Faulkner,, Mrs. Sarah B.	26,050
Faust, Andrew	1,200
Fay, Edwin	18,500
Fellows, Ann E	2,200
Fellows, George E	210
Fellows, Joshua E	660
Fensley, Mary	1,000
Fenton, Lucius C.	3,150
Fenton, Mary	1,100
Fenton, Patrick.	200
Field, John W.	4,100
Field, Manuel J.	1,520
Fillmore, George D	75
Fillmore, Ralph H.	1,600
Fillburn, Mary	80
First National Bank	13,300
Fish, Mrs. Ambrose H	1,600
Fiske, Samuel W, and Luella	5,015
Fitch, Charles S	240
Fitch, Edwin A.	4,200
Fitch, William, est	17,995
Fitch, William	900
Fitzgerald, Ellen	300
Fitzgerald, James	1,300
Fitzgerald, John	700
Fitzgerald, Maurice	750
Fitzgerald, Patrick	1,250
Fitzgerald, Patrick, 2d	700
Fitzgerald, Patrick, 3d	850
Fitzpatrick, John T	2,200
Fitzpatrick, Patrick	600
Fitzpatrick, Thomas B	200
Flaherty, Annie F	1,000

Fletcher, William S. 2,590
Flint, George 2,400
Flint, Mrs. Zerviah M 600
Fogarty, Patrick 400
Fogel, Ferdinand 1,000
Foley, Michael, est 300
Follett & Dearden 3,750
Fontaine & Reeves 5,250
Foote, Constant H 750
Forbes, Mary 800
Ford, George L 2,740
Ford, John H 2,700
Ford, Thomas 1,000
Ford, William P 300
Foster, Joel M 1,900
Fox, Hannah 500
Fox, Sarah M 3,800
Francis, Alvah 7,415
Francis, Alvah, & Co 2,100
Francis, John 800
Francis, John, 2d, est 2,425
Francis, Joseph 800
France, Robert A 350
Frazier, Lewis A 900
Frazier, Mrs. Nathan S 805
Frazier, Thomas M 750
Frazier, William 120
Freeman, Almira and Sister 330
Freeman, Samuel H 3,550
French, Mrs. Sarah F 10,050
Frink, Soloman A 3,175
Friswell, William 2,300
Fuller, Angeline M 9,250
Fuller, Chester 2,000
Fuller, Edward D 200
Fuller, Mrs. Eliza W 1,300
Fuller, George D., est 5,500
Fuller, Harriet L 2,300
Fuller, Joseph B. F 3,050
Fuller, Rebecca P 4,040
Fuller, Theodore 165
Fuller, Walter 2,450
Furlong, Moses 3,315
Fulton, William H 137

Gabrielle, Charles 3,925
Gager, Othniel 3,650
Gallagher, Patrick 150
Gallagher, William 1,100
Galligan, Patrick 450
Gallup, Charles D 1,105
Gallup, Harriet A 1,800
Gallup, Henry H 3,825
Gallup, Loren A 4,125
Galipp, Nelson 3,000
Gallup, William A 4,625
Gamble, Mrs. James 200
Gardner, Addison T 2,405
Gardner, Amy, est 1,250
Gardner, Anson 11,000
Gardner, Emeline 1,970
Gardner, Mrs. Edwin P 2,200
Gardner, Edwin B 2,040
Gardner, Edwin L 840
Gardner, Edwin P 4,700
Gardner, Erastus H 2,075
Gardner, Frederick L 4,325
Gardner, F. L. & C. H 800
Gardner, Harriet M 3,445
Gardner, Mrs. Harriet M 5,310
Gardner, Henry R 3,690
Gardner, Louisa F 250
Gardner, Lucius L 4,640
Gardner, Sidney, est 3,630
Garrity, James 680
Gates, Annie S 2,500
Gates, C. Henry 1,875
Gates, George G 4,100
Gates, Horace S 2,800
Gavitt, Mrs. Abby 1,600
Geduhdig, Gustave 2,500
Geer, Abram 800
Geer, Charles F 150
Geer, Elisha P 1,756
Geer, Ezra P 2,000
Geer, George W 13,420
Geer, George W., Jr 2,875
Geer, James L 7,000
Geer, Sidney L 13,725
Geer & Vergason 1,750
George, Mrs. Mary A 2,500
Gerber, Emil 1,000

Gernhard, Adam J.	$1,075
Gibbs, Edward N.	27,325
Gibbs, E. N. & H. B. Norton, trustees	6,000
Gibson, Catharine	1,400
Gibson, Owen	3,500
Gifford, Ira, est	—
Gifford, Stephen	3,000
Gilbert, Joseph W	1,029
Gilbert, Nathan S.	9,120
Gilbert, N. S. & Sons	13,575
Gilbert, S. Alpheus	200
Giles, Mrs. Abby A	3,500
Gill, Mrs. Elizabeth, est	800
Gilman, Mrs. Eliza, est	5,700
Gilmor, Ogden	120
Gilmartin, James	100
Gilmour, Bros.	6,150
Gilmour, David S	300
Gilmour, Mrs. Isabella S	1,500
Gilmour, James C.	600
Gilroy, Thomas	1,135
Glancey, Edward	835
Gleason, Dennis	935
Gleason, Jeremiah	100
Gleason, Thomas	1,425
Goff, Emily L	1,300
Goodrich, James T	500
Goodwin, Alice F	2,600
Goodwin & Parker	1,000
Gordon, Charles M	825
Gordon, Mrs. Samuel	220
Gordon, Thaddeus C., est	2,000
Gordon, William A	800
Gorman, George	1,720
Gorman, Richard	3,025
Gorton, Ira	1,000
Gotthelph, Moses	960
Gottlieb, Charles	340
Gough, Hugh	3,945
Gough, Matthew B	2,325
Gould, Augustus	2,025
Gould, George W	3,075
Gould, Lyman	6,850
Gould, Webster V	1,300
Gow, Elizabeth	3,000
Grace, Lucretia H	1,920
Grady, Frank D	2,000

Grady, Marcus F	$2,400
Grafton, James	4,400
Graham, James	2,000
Grant, Charles W	140
Gray, Mary D	2,520
Greene, Gardiner	3,910
Greene, Gardiner, Jr	825
Greene, J. Lloyd, est	31,400
Greene, Paul B	3,825
Greene, P. B. & Co	1,540
Greene, Sarah A	180
Greene, William M	2,000
Greene, William P.	38,350
Greenberg, Louis W	2,100
Greenhalgh, Robert	5,700
Greenman, Sarah L	2,550
Greenman, William H	80
Greenwood, James	6,000
Griffin, Frank E	1,875
Griffin, Patrick	200
Grimes, William	2,500
Griswold, Henry E.	1,800
Griswold, Joseph A	2,130
Gulliver, Daniel F	30,080
Guy, John H	1,300
Hagberg, Andrew	1,000
Hale, Rebecca B	1,100
Halliday, Daniel	800
Hall, Benjamin	7,450
Hall Bros	16,500
Hall, Daniel	2,620
Hall, George	8,250
Hall, Henry	1,200
Hall, William	2,595
Halliday, Janet	3,328
Hallahan, Jeremiah	800
Hallahan, Mary	350
Hallahan, Patrick	1,300
Hallam, Henry W., est	825
Halsey, Jeremiah	18,600
Hammond, Henry K.	7,500
Hanrihan, John	820
Hanrihan, Patrick	720
Handrihan, Thomas	900
Handrihan, William	900
Hanna, Eliza	1,320

Hanna, Jane	$960
Hanniford, Michael	1,000
Hannis, Benjamin C.	840
Harder, George W.	400
Harland, Abby L.	8,605
Harland, Edward	75
Harrigan, John	1,200
Harrigan, William	800
Harrington, Patrick	400
Harris, Frank P.	125
Harris, George W.	800
Harris, Sarah W.	100
Hartigan, John	400
Hartigan, Mary	400
Hartigan, Richard	909
Hartley, William	7,200
Hartley, Wm., & C. McNamara	1,800
Harvey, Mary	1,540
Harwood & Co.	8,400
Haskell, Charles C.	5,205
Haskell, Henry E.	5,675
Hastings, Charles	1,725
Haven, Robert M., est	2,500
Hayes, John	500
Hazard, Almira J.	1,420
Hazlehurst, Edward, est	360
Healey, Margaret	900
Hebard, A. Y., heirs	5,400
Hempstead, William S.	5,875
Henderson, James, 1st	2,500
Henderson, James, 2d	1,055
Henderson, Joseph H.	1,600
Henderson, Margaret	880
Henderson, Robert	3,200
Henderson, William	2,985
Hennesy, Martin	450
Herr, J. D.	3,100
Herrick, Burrill A.	3,500
Herrick, Harris E.	4,000
Herrick, Robert A.	5,150
Hess, George	4,015
Hewett & Setchell	6,000
Hibbard, William H.	2,348
Hickey, Catherine	800
Hickey, Daniel D.	2,150
Higgins, Silas	2,000
Higgins, Werter C.	$4,100
Higgins, William W.	1,200
Higney, Margaret	180
Hill, Charles W.	1,365
Hill, Fanny, est	1,400
Hill, Hiram	3,500
Hill, Hiram C.	1,800
Hill, Ira J.	1,905
Hill, John L.	1,250
Hill, Mary C.	2,000
Hill, Mrs. Susan	1,200
Hilton & Bidwell	8,000
Hilton, C. Otis	2,000
Hinchey, Patrick	920
Hinckley, Amos P., est	1,800
Hinckley, Betsy A.	2,000
Hinckley, Eliza C.	2,000
Hinckley, Joann	1,100
Hirsch & Co.	3,000
Hiscox, B. H.	1,000
Hislop, James	1,200
Hislop, Porteous & Mitchell	35,150
Hoar, William	1,300
Hefferman, Julia A.	1,570
Hogan, Andrew	540
Hogan, James	
Holbrook, Charles S.	2,800
Holbrook, Supply T.	320
Holden, Thomas	2,400
Holdroyd, Andrew L.	2,940
Holdroyd, Job	1,200
Holland, Daniel	700
Holman, Mary	1,000
Holloway Bros.	3,715
Holm, Peter	840
Holmes, Dwight R.	1,600
Holmes, Emily M.	500
Holmes, Henry	2,500
Holmes, Thomas A.	50
Holt, Charles H.	950
Holt, Daniel, est	3,100
Holt, Martha G.	1,040
Holyoke, Mary B.	6,500
Hood Fire Arms Co.	21,000

Hooker, Jonathan W. 4,550
Hoolihan, Timothy 900
Hopkins & Allen M'f'g Co. 52,000
Hopkins, Charles W 3,450
Hopkins, Sally C. 900
Hopkins, Samuel S. 3,935
Horan, Ann 700
Hourigan, Ellen, est. 1,800
Hourigan, Michael 3,070
Houston, James 6,650
Hovey, James A 6,825
Hovey, Laurina B. 4,239
Howe Machine Co. 400
Howe, Samuel G. & William R 1,950
Howie, Susan M. 2,650
Howard, Edward 120
Hubbard, A. H. & Co. 99,800
Hubbard, Daniel R. 2,200
Hubbard, Harriet F. 2,400
Hubbard, James L. 32,050
Hubbard, Mrs. Sarah L. 6,530
Hubbell, A. S. & L. B 2,850
Hubbell, Richard M 400
Hughes, George F. 250
Hughes, Maria 1,400
Hulbert, Charles H. 7,925
Hull, Charles A. 500
Hull, Sarah A 6,301
Hunter, Edward 1,490
Hunter, Hugh 725
Hunter, John A. 2,175
Hunter, Joseph 880
Hunter, Stephen 350
Huntington, Amelia M., est 4,800
Huntington, Benjamin, est. 2,150
Huntington, Edward A. 5,927
Huntington, Edward P., est 13,825
Huntington, Mrs. E. R. 11,845
Huntington, Mrs. E. R., guardian 10,000
Huntington, H. L. 600
Huntington, Hezekiah 9,175
Huntington, Jedediah 16,150
Huntington J. L. W 2,000
Huntington, J. M. & Co 25,000
Huntington, John G. & Co. 29,500
Huntington, Malvina A. 6,286
Huntington, Palatiah W 550
Huntington, Roscoe 11,750
Huntington, Miss Sarah J 7,125
Hurlburt, Ruth C. 800
Hurley, James and Mary 2,700
Hutchison, William 750
Hyde, Amasa L. 1,900
Hyde, Burrill W. 3,350
Hyde, Eunice E 1,500
Hyde, George R 20,640
Hyde, Harlan 3,125
Hyde, Lewis A 20,250
Hyde, Lewis A., guardian 960
Hyde, Solomon 300
Hyland, Ann 800
Hynds, Bernard 450

Irons, George W 135

Jackson, Frederick S. 50
Jackson, Simon C 700
James, Charles D. 5,200
James, Julia B 240
Jenkins, Margaret 965
Jennings, Mrs. C. W. 3,000
Jennings, John 1,750
Jennings, Mason P 3,400
Jennings, William H 9,025
Jewett, Mrs. Eliza C. 1,200
Jewett, Laban R 8,435
Jillson, George W 1,700
Jones, Caroline F. 3,000
Jones, George T. 1,176
Jones, J. Horace 1,210
Jones, Mrs. Lucy S 10,500
Jones, Rees D. & Son 1,200
Jones, William A 2,100
Jordan, Timothy 240
Johnson, Charles C 26,645
Johnson, Frank 33,100
Johnson, Mrs. F. A. C. 3,500
Johnson, Mrs. Jane 600
Johnson, Jerry 800
Johnson, Oliver L. Jr 50
Johnson, Maria E 24,500
Johnson, Thomas and Eliza 900
Johnson, Frank, trustee, Elizabeth D. Child, est 575

Johnson, Frank, trustee, L. F. S. Foster, est 20,840
Johnson, Frank, trustee, Mary L. Drake 1,150
Johnson, Frank, trustee, Charles Farnsworth, est 3,080
Johnson, Frank, trustee, H. K. Huntington, est 1,775
Johnson, Frank, trustee, Zachary Huntington, est 28,319
Johnson, Frank, trustee, Joseph Lanman, est 5,000
Johnson, Frank, trustee, Maria L. Morgan, est 5,600
Johnson, Frank, trustee, Luther Pellet, est 10,500
Johnson, Frank, trustee, Maria H. Perkins, est 200
Johnson, Frank, trustee, Horace Walker, est 5,300
Johnson, Frank, and James D. Mowry, trustees of estate of David Smith 34,850

Kampf, George 1,500
Kane, John 1,000
Kane, Mrs. Margaret 700
Kealdes, A. B. 650
Keating, Cornelius 1,030
Kearney, Lawrence, ... 700
Keegan, Patrick 700
Keeley, David 4,600
Keenan, Bernard 1,200
Keenan, Felix 4,000
Keenan, Patrick 775
Keep, John H 5,150
Kehr, John Adam, est 1,500
Kehr, Jacob 2,000
Kegwin, Elinor C. 3,300
Kelleher, Cornelius 1,050
Keileher, Hugh 1,200
Kelly, John H. 12,150
Kellogg, John C. 3,500
Kelly, Barney 1,100
Kelly, Daniel 1,025
Keily, Henry 1,950
Kelly, John, est 600
Kelly, John, 2nd 800
Kelly, John 45
Kelly, John B. 395
Kelly, John W. 1,000
Kelly, Mrs. Mary, est 1,100
Kelly, Patrick 850
Kelly, Patrick F. 900
Kelly, Richard C. 2,975
Kelly, Robert 720
Kelly, Simon 1,225
Kelly, Thomas 750
Kelly, Timothy 8,700
Kempner, Jacob 400
Kennedy, Dennis 450
Kennedy, John 700
Kennedy, William, est 770
Kenyon, Charles H. 11,200
Keppler, S. P. 400
Kerley, Catherine 330
Kerrigan, Margaret 840
Keough, John 1,400
Kieley, John 700
Kies, George A. 100
Kies, George W. 10,400
Kilcolum, James, est 240
Kilrow, Mary 2,400
Kilrow, Michael 900
Kilroy, Alice 700
Kilroy, Thomas 1,750
Kilroy, William 1,100
Kimball, Amos L., est 1,640
Kimball, James 400
Kimball, John 2,000
Kind, Joseph 1,000
King, Charles J 7,678
King, Edward, est 800
Kingsbury, Henry A 5,350
Kingsley, Eleazer 2,050
Kingsley, Joseph K. 1,250
Kingsley, Luke 1,080
Kingsley, William L 675
Kinney, Albert W. 3,075
Kinney, Ann M 1,000
Kinney, Elijah C 1,450
Kinney, Emily 1,800

Kinney, George	$20,575
Kinney, Harlan	95
Kinney, Martin	500
Kinney, Jacob W., est	15,250
Kinney, Mason	15,250
Kirker, Mary	900
Klien, Frederick L	1,600
Knight, Mary C. S	6,895
Korn, Charles F	3,630
Konin, Adolph	330
Ladd, N. L. M	137
Ladd, Rufus M., est	2,400
Laighton Brothers	500
Lamb, George W	1,500
Lamb, Jefferson	3,000
Lamb, M. V. B	7,325
Lamb, Orlando J	1,425
Lambert, Peter	1,230
Landolt, Jost	1,400
Landon, James O	— –
Lane Brothers	600
Lang, Frederick	1,500
Langeliar, Frank	3,450
Langdon, Mrs. Jane	220
Lanman, Abby T	6,750
Lanman, Mary E	500
Lanman, Peter, agent	905
Lanman, William C	18,225
Lapierre, Arnoud	3,005
Lathrop, Arthur D	5,750
Lathrop, E. H	1,900
Lathrop, George, est	4,137
Lathrop, Jabez S	1,580
Lathrop, James	2,000
Lathrop, John A	350
Lathrop, J. L. & F. L	325
Lathrop, Mary A	3,300
Lathrop, Mary B	1,200
Lathrop, William B	8,550
Lathrop, William R	2,815
Lathrop & Carey	2,000
Latour, R. F	1,350
Lavender, Mary J	$1,845
Lawrence, John P., est	1,275
Lay, Charles W	99
Leach, Emeline	7,500
Leach, James J	6,415
Leach, Laura S	2 075
Leahy, Thomas	800
Learned, Bela P	2,510
Learned, Bela P., trustee	1,000
Learned, Ebenezer	9,075
Leary, Thomas	60
Leary, Timothy, est	590
Leary, Timothy	800
Leavens, Frances J	9,750
Leavens, Francis J	5,500
Leavens, F. J., trustee	4,000
Leavens, Josephine M	1,275
Leavens, Kirk H	7,880
Leavens, Lucy G	1,175
Leavens, Martha M	2,625
Lee, Charles, est	10,750
Lee, Ira, est	500
Lee, F. B., est	7,500
Lee, Henry P	4,205
Lee, Lyman W	1,600
Lee, Minnie E	110
Lee & Osgood	31,000
Leffingwell, Charles H	2,700
Lemas, Antone	910
Lennon, Patrick	264
Leo, Patrick	1,300
Lester, Amos	5,135
Lester, Austin A	2,000
Lester, Daniel M	2,775
Lester, Elizabeth W	9,000
Lester & Wesley	5,000
Levaggi, Antonia	1,265
Lewis, David M., est	2,200
Lewis, Elizabeth D	2,400
Lewis, George D	1,400
Lewis, Joseph P	4,500
Lewis, John W	150
Lewis, Maxson	10,000
Lewis, Russell	2,425

Leyrer, Jacob	$1,125
Lillebridge, Christopher G	1,200
Lillebridge, Daniel	2,700
Lillebridge, Daniel & Thurston	6,025
Lillebridge, Greene	6,075
Lillebridge, Joseph W	3,020
Lillebridge, Thomas A	2,895
Lincoln, George S	1,300
Lindsey, James, est	450
Linnehan, John	1,400
Linnell, Edward H	185
Linnell, Jonathan E	6,625
Lippitt, Costello	2,825
Lippitt, Costello, guardian	2,200
Lippitt, George	3,750
Lippitt, George & Co	8,175
Lippitt, Norris G	4,200
Lonergan, William	1,320
Looby, Michael	1,100
Loomis, Abigail B	3,500
Loomis, George, est	3,000
Loomis, Lottie and Clara	3,850
Losee, Elijah M	2,050
Lotter, Grace	1,300
Lovell Brothers	2,575
Lovell, Joseph H	2,000
Lowden, Mrs. Mary	500
Lucas, Benjamin and Solomon	2,100
Lucas, Joseph H	2,570
Lucas, Noah	3,050
Lucas, Solomon	10,800
Luce, Mrs. John C.	2,200
Lucey, Daniel, est	1,000
Lucey, William and Amos	240
Lumis & Sutton	915
Lumsden, James	120
Lutts, Charles	1,700
Lyman, Daniel D	50
Lyman, John D	5,180
Lynch, John	500
Lynch, Michael	1,320
Lynch, Patrick	1,200
Lyons, Bridget	375
Mabrey, Mary E	$500
Mack, Cornelius, est	1,200
Macomber, George	165
Madden, Hugh	900
Mahoney, Mary	900
Mahoney, Patrick	1,700
Maine, Albert B	2,745
Malone, Daniel	525
Manahan, John	1,500
Mangan, John	1,680
Manning, William D	6,400
Manwaring, John	6,345
Maples, Annie M	4,300
Maples, Charles	5,430
Maples, Charles, conservator	1,320
Maples, David L and B. W	1,900
Maples, Leonard T	1,550
Maples, Mrs. Nancy H	15,626
Maples, Stephen L	200
Mara, Michael	700
Mara, Patrick	800
Marshall, Rufus W	2,965
Martin, Alexander J	82
Martin, George H	3,775
Martin, Peter	300
Martin, William J	1,200
Mason, Andrew, est	780
Mason, Marilla H	624
Mason, William H	13,300
Mathews, Arthur	2,030
Mathews, Mrs. Eliza	1,100
Mathews, James	900
Mathews, William	700
Mathews, William J	1,200
Mathewson, Darius R., est	17,050
Mathewson, Laura E	150
McCabe, Margaret	700
McCabe, Michael	1,200
McCabe, Thomas	625
McCaffrey, James	975
McCaffrey, Peter	1,280
McCall, James	900
McCall, Mrs. Stephen T	900
McChesney, Charles	9,105
McClellan, George	1,702
McClellan, Grace	1,000

McCloud, John 1,400
McCloud, William 1,025
McClune, Dennis 2,640
McClure, George 1,295
McCormick, John 770
McCormick, Daniel 250
McCormick, Mary 210
McCoy, James 156
McCoy, Sarah 540
McCune, Patrick 1,700
McCurdy, Theodore F 14,350
McDermot., Michael ..... —
McDonald, Donald 1,300
McDonald, Thomas, est 1,200
McDougall, John 900
McFadden, Richard 2,050
McGarrity, Thomas 720
McGarry, Thomas 900
McGee, Arthur 1,000
McGee, Mrs. Sarah A 2,500
McGinnis, John 1,200
McGinnis, Patrick 800
McGrath, John 700
McJennett, John 2,400
McKay, George 195
McKiernan, Margaret 900
McKnight, John 1,200
McLaughlin, Andrew 2,290
McLaughlin, George 800
McLaughlin, Patrick 1,300
McMahon, Edward 1,000
McMahon, John 800
McManus, Barney 330
McManus, Eliza 840
McNamara Brothers 5,075
McNamara, Cornelius 935
McNamara, C. and J. R. 2,550
McNamara, John R. 600
McNamara, John R., guardian 1,500
McNamara, Michael 500
McNamara, Michael J 800
McNamara, Patrick 1,500
McNamara & O'Hearn 950
McNamara & Pratt 8,650
McNelly, John, est 1,067
McNelly, Peter, est 1,300
McNelly, William 550
McNickle, Alexander 1,600
McNickle, John 700
McNulty, James E. 1,800
McQuirk, Michael 1,525
McVicker, Daniel 1,700
McWhirr, Robert ..... —
McWilliams, John 1,600
Mead, Benjamin F. 1,230
Meech, Dwight T. 2,030
Meech, James M. 6,050
Meech, John H., est 3,000
Meech, Levi W. 4,870
Meech, Lizzie 400
Meech, Stephen B 5,175
Meehan, Francis 700
Meehan, John, 1st 1,325
Meehan, John 2,125
Meeker, Miss Henrietta 10,400
Megary, Richard P. 1,250
Menck, Charles 360
Mershon, Jacob B 8,600
Messinger, Robert G. 600
Metzger, Caspar 700
Metzger, Jacob 800
Millea, Andrew 800
Miller, Avery N 1,950
Miller, Mrs. Frances 1,250
Miller, Henry 2,800
Miller, John P. 1,650
Mills, Robert 600
Millington, Louisa M. 8,250
Miner, Charles H. 1,300
Miner, Edwin B. 9,200
Miner, James P. 1,500
Minor, Solomon C. 548
Mitchell, Albert G. 8,875
Mitchell Brothers 28,000
Mitchell, Frank A 6,075
Mitchell, Mrs. Henry 3,600
Mitchell, John 19,675
Mitchell, Joseph T. 100
Mitchell, Mrs. Thomas 2,200
Moloney, Mrs. Julia, est 6,250
Monaher, Michael 2,500
Monroe, John C 90
Montgomery, Hugh 2,900

Moore, Christopher C.	1,500
Moore, Ellen	1,500
Moore, George H	3,700
Moore, John M	4,125
Moran, Michael and Sarah E	5,734
Moran, Samuel	1,100
Morgan, Ann	1,650
Morgan, Mrs. Frances M	1,100
Morgan, John A	8,900
Morgan, John A , 2d	5,000
Morgan, John C	2,075
Morgan, Mabel A., est	4,000
Morgan, Roswell, heirs	2,000
Moriarty, Daniel	1,050
Moriarty, James	3,000
Moriarty, John	720
Moriarty, Stephen	1,500
Morris, Henry	2,250
Morris, Patrick	770
Morris, Thomas	300
Morrison, J. Henry	3,000
Morrison, John H.	2,150
Morse, Maria and Eunice P.	900
Morse, Maurice E.	300
Mossman, Mrs. E. P.	11,340
Mowry, Ezra W.	3,750
Mowry, James D., trustee	4,000
Mulcahey, Thomas	1,200
Mulholland, John	357
Muller Brothers	330
Murphy, Anthony J. & Co.	440
Murphy, Bridget	720
Murphy, Bridget, 2nd	2,800
Murphy, Daniel D.	840
Murphy, Dennis D.	220
Murphy, James	3,540
Murphy, James, 2nd	900
Murphy, Jeremiah	624
Murphy, John, 1st	960
Murphy, John, 2nd	400
Murphy, John P.	1,195
Murphy, J. P. & T. C.	1,875
Murphy, Mary	1,900
Murphy, Michael, 1st	450
Murphy, Michael, 2nd	1,100
Murphy, Michael, 3rd	3,900
Murphy, Michael D.	1,100
Murphy, Richard	1,700
Murphy, Susannah	960
Murphy, Wm. J. & J. W	500
Murray, James	1,100
Murray, Michael	600
Murray, Peter	1,200
Murray, Stuart	1,100
Murtha, Mary	2,800
Murtagh, Patrick F.	1,000
Musgrove, Joseph	1,225
Mussell, Mary	800
Myers, Austin W.	7,400
Myers, James H.	720
Myers & Bailey	15,500
Nagle, John	1,050
Neil, William	1,400
Nevin, John	2,230
Newman, Thomas	1,300
Newton, James W	200
Newton, John M	1,100
Newton, Palmer, est	6,285
Nichols, Franklin	17,250
Nichols, Frank W	1,650
Nichols, Hezekiah	4,550
Nichols, Mrs. Louisa L.	2,500
Noble, David	600
Nolan, George	1,200
Nolan, James	750
Nolan, James F	400
Nolan, Keeran	525
Nolan, Mary	420
Nolan, Michael	1,870
Nolan, Thomas J.	880
Norton, George B.	1,200
Norton, Henry A	225
Norton, Henry B.	33,950
Norton, H. B. & J. B. Colgate, trustees	15,000
Norton, Timothy P., est	11,150
Norwich Belt Mfg. Co.	13,520
Norwich Bleaching, Dyeing & Printing Co.	310,500
Norwich City Gas Co.	125,000
Norwich Lock Mfg. Co	38,500
Norwich Falls Pistol Co	15,000

Norwich Plate Co. 300
Norwich Savings Society 31,400
Norwich, N. L. & W. H. S. B. Co. 6,000
Norwich & N. Y. Trans. Co. 500,000
Norwich Water Power Co. 86,800
Norwich Wooden Co. 77,500
Norwich Horse R. R. Co. 660
Noss, George 1,000
Noss, J. Adam 500
Noss, William 17,275
Noyes, Mrs. B. G. 2,250
Noyes, Caleb H. 1,050
Noyes, Courtland 1,050
Noyes, Jesse D. 5,000
Noyes & Davis 2,200

Oakes, Edward 82
Oatley, Thomas, est 700
Obenaur, Martin, est 2,400
Occum Company 16,675
O'Brien, Clara S. 150
O'Brien, E. O., est, & John Brewster 5,000
O'Brien, Jeremiah 450
O'Brien, John J 700
O'Brien, Thomas 900
O'Brien, Thomas, 2nd 2,600
O'Connell, Ann, est 1,080
O'Connell, Bridget 1,000
O'Connell, Daniel 110
O'Connor, Patrick J 5,900
O'Donavan, James 1,650
Ogden, William 2,400
O'Hearn, Joanna 440
O'Keefe, Edmund 880
O'Kelly, James 1,680
O'Kelly, Timothy 120
O'Mahoney, Patrick 2,240
O'Neil, Ann 540
O'Neil, Abby 1,500
O'Neil, Catharine 600
O'Neil, Daniel, 1st 1,300
O'Neil, Daniel, 2nd 600
O'Neil, Jane 330
O'Neil, Patrick, 1st 82
O'Neil, Patrick, 2nd 400
O'Neil, Thomas 900
O'Neil, William 1,000
O'Rourke, Michael 700
O'Rourke, Michael, est 480
Osborne, Thomas 500
Osgood & Allen 900
Osgood, Artemas 3,500
Osgood, Charles, est 45,300
Osgood, Mrs. Charles 20,640
Osgood, Charles H 34,000
Osgood, C. H. & F. L. 2,900
Osgood, Frederick L 20,690
Osgood, Hugh H 16,050
Osgood, William C 19,165
O'Sullivan, Patrick 1,100
O'Sullivan, Peter 650
O'Sullivan, Richard 840
Ossawan Mills Co. 9,000
Otis, Amos T 10,550

Paddock, Lewis S. 500
Page Steam Heating Co. 6,400
Page, Wm. H., Wood Type Co. 17,500
Page, Elnor E. 2,000
Palmer, Benjamin H 9,225
Palmer, Charles H., 1st 1,970
Palmer, Charles H., 2nd 870
Palmer, Edwin 4,475
Palmer, George F 1,325
Palmer, Henry 5,675
Palmer, Henry, 2nd 3,425
Palmer, Henry F 5,875
Palmer, Herbert I 1,300
Palmer, Mrs. Isabella 1,700
Palmer, John C 9,950
Palmer, Lucy A 2,200
Palmer, Robert J 2,500
Palmer, William S 180
Palmer & Brown 7,000
Paracenti, John 180
Park, Albert F. 25
Park, Cyrus B 3,675
Park, Hattie C. 1,000
Park, John D 7,945
Park, Joseph H 800

Park, Thomas 1,200
Park, Webster, est 3,650
Park & Harris 700
Parker, Ebenezer F 3,025
Parker, Guilford 1,500
Parker, Henry L 8,740
Parker, John H., est 1,500
Parker, Robert B 2,150
Parkhurst, Chester 770
Parkhurst, Elias 1,391
Parkinson, Rosanna, est 1,200
Parlin, Simon R 1,600
Parsons, Benjamin F 1,210
Patterson, Margaret M 1,200
Peale, Charles S 2,500
Peale, Henry, Jr 1,500
Pease, William 2,900
Peck, Anthony, Jr 380
Peck, Mrs. Ellen S 3,600
Peck, Ira L 3,070
Peck, John H 10,400
Peck, Seth L 3,825
Peckham, Albertus 3,875
Peckham, Isaac M., est 300
Peckham, James 2,150
Peckham, Lucius 1,080
Peckham, Restcome 2,345
Pellett, Elijah M 1,200
Pendleton, Charles M 6,567
Pendleton, Chas. M., conservator 1,400
Perkins, Charles H 975
Perkins, Clement L 100
Perkins, Daniel W 1,700
Perkins, Donald L. and wife 1,200
Perkins, George L 10,675
Perkins, John C 15,305
Perkins, John T 1,965
Perkins, John T. & Co 850
Perkins, Jonathan 3,135
Perkins, Sarah H 575
Perkins, Thomas A 2,700
Perkins, William M 1,400
Perkins, William S. C 7,925
Perkins, Willis D 1,850
Perry, Elisha 150
Perry, Harriet G., est 2,500
Pettis, Jabez M 150
Pettit, Julia and Sarah Bowen, heirs 1,400
Phillips, Dwight L 1,500
Phillips, Dwight L., Jr 50
Phillips, Henry T 60
Phillips, John P 1,615
Phinney, Elisha 575
Pierce, George 6,475
Pierce, Lucy A 726
Pierce, Moses 13,125
Pierce, William B 3,360
Pierson, Martin V 1,270
Pitcher, Albert 4,055
Pitcher, Albert H 1,850
Pitcher, A. H. & H. A 5,150
Pitcher, Elijah W 3,385
Pitcher, George W 1,250
Pitcher, Henry A 150
Pitcher, Garrad G 7,340
Platt, Mrs. Charles B 33,850
Plant, Abraham 1,500
Plant, Isaac 1,300
Plant, Joseph 12,000
Plummer, Richard H 10,650
Ponemah Mills 908,000
Pope, Jonathan A 8,025
Popple, Charles T 75
Porteous, John 7,425
Porter, Heman B 1,950
Porter, Selden T 137
Potter, Charles H 4,600
Potter, Daniel B 420
Potter, Henry H 1,195
Potter, Henry T 9,620
Potter, John 3,600
Potter, M. A 1,000
Potter, Wm. P 4,575
Potter, Wm. P., Jr 2,000
Potter, Wm. R 1,255
Powelson, John H 2,800
Powers Brothers 217
Pratt, George H 1,100
Pratt, Mary A 3,800
Pratt, Melissa S 600
Pratt, Michael 1,000
Pratt, Patrick 1,152
Pray, Ellen 700

Name	Amount
Prentice, Amos W.	32,525
Prentice, A. W., trustee estate John Dunham	3,300
Prentice, A. W. & Co.	25,400
Prentice, Arthur C.	1,200
Prentice, Catharine	800
Prentice, Harriet A., est.	5,000
Prentice, Samuel	4,935
Preston Brothers	3,000
Price, Zebulon R., est	1,500
Prior, Charles R., Mrs.	1,425
Proctor, Alexander	1,600
Quinn, James	600
Quinlan, Patrick	1,100
Quirk, Ellen	250
Quito (Corteaux), Joseph D	297
Rafferty, Ann	495
Rafferty, Patrick J	1,100
Rallion, Calista C.	5,000
Rallion, Herman D	2,050
Ramage, Charles T.	2,250
Ramage, John	1,100
Randall, Lyman W., est	7,665
Randall, Sally A	175
Ransom, Charlotte M.	3,900
Ransom, George M	7,620
Raphael, Ellis	1,500
Rathbone, Abel	2,825
Rathbone, Charles A.	1,000
Rathbone, Mrs. E. L.	2,000
Rathbone, Jewett D.	480
Rathbone, Russell	8,550
Rathbone, Beriah S.	4,060
Rathbone, William A	500
Ratigan, John	2,600
Ratigan, Thomas, Jr	1,100
Rawson, Calvin G	31,675
Rawson, Luther S	7,600
Rawson & Whipple	10,000
Rawson, William F	200
Ray, Albert A	5,025
Ray, Daniel L.	1,000
Ray, Edward	3,100
Ray, Frederick G.	950
Ray, G. Avery	— —
Ray, Henry D	1,775
Ray, Mary H.	1,500
Ray, Stephen B.	2,085
Raymond, George C.	450
Raymond, Theodore	26,400
Raymond, William	240
Regan, Cornelius, est.	400
Regan, Timothy	650
Reardon, Michael	3,547
Reid, James A.	700
Reid & Hughes	18,000
Revell, John	2,000
Revell, Robert	7,500
Revell, Sweetman	200
Reynolds, Catharine	550
Reynolds, Chas. L. H.	379
Reynolds, Edward K.	1,700
Reynolds, George	2,300
Reynolds, Henry L.	10,710
Reynolds, Mary A.	900
Reynolds, Oliver H.	16,100
Reynolds, Thomas L.	3,000
Rice, Frank G	800
Rice & Rich	564
Richards, Charles L.	58,035
Richmond, John B.	847
Richmond Stove Company	78,100
Richmond, William H. S.	1,820
Richter, Frederick	5,000
Ricker, William B.	2,060
Ridgeway, Thomas J.	15,150
Riley, Ann	750
Ring, David, est	1,600
Ring, David P.	1,400
Ring, Michael B	1,600
Riordan, Thomas	360
Ripley, Hannah G.	20,915
Ripley, Hezekiah	1,650
Ripley, James L. Mrs., est.	8,645
Ripley, Jane	3,850
Risley, Sarah E.	1,600

Ritchie, James 2,500
Roach, Edward 600
Roarke, Michael 1,400
Roath, Chas. E 1,000
Roath, Edmund D 46,775
Roath, Edwin A. 8,825
Roath, Elizabeth 1,430
Roath, H. Hobart 11,135
Roath, Jane & Mary 1,400
Roath, Lewis P 3,750
Roath, William 1,075
Robbins, Zebulon, est 27,630
Robbins, Zebulon, Jr 2,000
Robinson, Ellen 440
Robinson, Frank A 1,190
Robinson, N. D. Mrs 800
Robinson, William C 1,200
Rockwell, Mary W 52,915
Rogers, Andrew 1,100
Rogers, Alfred D 1,600
Rogers, C. B. & Co 112,700
Rogers, Carrie 5,465
Rogers, Charles J 200
Rogers, Elijah H 800
Rogers, Harriet F 600
Rogers, Harriet M 565
Rogers, Henry 1,400
Rogers, James D 2,870
Rogers, Joab B 2,090
Rogers, J. Frank 146
Rogers, Lewis 1,500
Rogers, Louis H 1,800
Rogers, Porter 2,360
Rogers, Sarah B 2,000
Rogers, Sarah E 1,700
Rogers, William D 6,955
Rogers, William P 2,042
Rohan, James 600
Roman, Michael 300
Rollinson, Joseph 1,701
Rose, Eleanor M 1,800
Rose, Peleg G. & Co 1,320
Rose, Reuben P 1,395
Ross, William M 3,000
Rourke, John 10,500
Royce, A. Irving 3,450
Ruby, David T 8,450
Ruch, Andrew 350
Rudd, Catharine W 800
Rudd, Hezekiah F 23,450
Rood, Henry B 895
Ruggles, Henry 15,650
Ruggles, Miami 1,200
Ryan, John A 1,100
Ryan, Mary 600
Ryan, Patrick 400
Ryan, Thomas E 9,955
Ryan, T. E. & Co 660
Ryan, William 600

Safford, Morgan 8,800
Safford, M. & Co 2,000
Salomon, Louis 3,300
Samuel, Max 1,206
Saunders, Henry J 200
Saxton, Lewis J 3,015
Sayles, Thomas D 18,275
Scholfield, John 1,500
Scott, Charles W., Jr 2,720
Scott, John H 3,650
Scott, Welcome S., est 3,755
Scoville, Henry W 400
Second Congregational Church 2,300
Sears, Myron 3,600
Seidel, Henry 1,000
Selden, Joseph 5,585
Sellick, Charles A 2,200
Semple, James 1,700
Semple, James W 880
Seney, J. T. & T 550
Senft, Albert 1,865
Service, James 1,600
Service, John 1,500
Service, John P 2,740
Service, Peter, est 500
Setchell, Charles F 10,475
Setchell, George C 1,600
Sevin, John F 7,775
Sevin, N. Douglass 8,000
Seymour, Matilda 900
Shahan, Peter P 1,050

Name	Amount
Shailer, Francis A	1,300
Shanley, Mary J	1,000
Shannon, J. B. & Co	22,700
Shaw, John B	5,600
Shaw, Daniel B	500
Shea, Mrs. Elizabeth	170
Shea, James T	330
Shea, Jeremiah	1,895
Shea, John	2,700
Shea, Murty	1,039
Shea, Murty, Jr	90
Shea, Patrick, est	3,000
Sheehan, Michael	720
Sheehan, Patrick	1,080
Sheffield, Mrs. Julia A	1,400
Sheffield, Sally	500
Sheridan, John	900
Sheridan, Mathew	1,540
Sherman, Abial B	4,600
Sherman, Abial W	3,500
Sherman, Mrs. Betsey	1,600
Sherman, Mrs. Eunice	6,560
Sherman, Horace M	2,125
Sherman, John E	2,250
Sherman, Rufus C	2,800
Sherman, Thomas S	1,525
Sherman, William L	3,100
Shetucket Company	374,450
Shew, William K	330
Shields, Wm. H	6,475
Sholes, Sanford H	4,425
Shugrue, Daniel	1,000
Shugrue, John, 1st	860
Shugrue, John, 2d	1,030
Shugrue, John J	900
Shugrue, Roger	600
Sibley, Rufus	6,500
Sibley Machine Co	6,200
Silvia, Frank	900
Silvia, John	1,300
Silvia, Joseph	1,025
Simpson, John	1,000
Silcox, Henry E	2,600
Simonds, Christopher C	600
Sims, Jeremiah	1,450
Singer S. M. Co	900
Skeesacks, E. L	700
Skelly, Bridget	960
Skelly, Patrick	920
Skelly, Thomas	600
Skinner, Henry	1,275
Slater, John F	36,675
Slater, Mrs. M. L	22,250
Slocum, Elisha P	2,800
Small, Nathan	5,100
Smiley, Robert J	1,500
Smith, Mrs. Achsah D	2,800
Smith, A. F., est	10,450
Smith, Annie E. and Abbie M	13,165
Smith, Albert D	100
Smith, Ada W	5,000
Smith, Bartlett	960
Smith, B. C., est	2,775
Smith, Charles H	418
Smith, Catharine P	1,200
Smith, George S	9,075
Smith, George W	6,325
Smith, Hiram	1,800
Smith, James L	1,630
Smith, Joseph A., heirs	1,850
Smith, Joseph F	3,210
Smith, J. Hunt	3,860
Smith, Jeremiah	220
Smith, Mrs. L. T. and Lizzie Jewett	3,555
Smith, Margaret	1,400
Smith, Mary Ann	1,400
Smith, Nehemiah	400
Smith, Owen S	4,334
Smith, Palmer	11,625
Smith, Paul	50
Smith, Sidney C	1,100
Smith, Sidney L	750
Smith, Thomas H	2,500
Smith, Welcome A	1,000
Smith, William	2,765
Smith, William, 2d	915
Smith, William Asa	50
Smith, William G	600
Smith, William R	1,350
Smith & Beckwith	4,730
Smith & Gilbert	5,000
Snell, Ennis B	1,200
Souter, Robert	2,550
Spafford, George C	2,500

Name	Amount
Spalding, Charles	58,125
Spalding, Ch. & F. Johnson, trustees	5,870
Spalding, Chas. W	4,000
Spalding, Harvey	115
Spalding & Allen	1,000
Spear, Levi, est	30,000
Spencer, Joseph B	4,270
Spicer, Francina	440
Spicer, Worthington H	1,450
Spivery, Thomas A	1,000
Spooner, Charles A., est	2,000
Sprague, Seth L	4,050
Sprague, William, est	3,125
Standish, John G	2,600
Standish, Nathan, est	4,000
Stanley, James	320
Stanton, George P	3,500
Stanton, James	800
Stanton, Jane G	150
Stanton, John	367
Stanton, John R	10,130
Stanton, Nathan L., est	360
Stanton, Robert P	1,800
Stanton, Turner	9,650
Stanton, William N	165
Stanton & Tyler	1,350
Staples, Elias W	3,095
Stapleton, John, est	300
Stapleton, Mrs. Louisa	500
Stark, C. E.	192
Starkweather, Jacob F	418
Starr, Edwin J	1,000
Staubly, John	1,850
Stead, Angel	5,800
Steadman, Joseph R	1,600
Steadman, J. W. and others	6,000
Steiner, John	27,520
Sterry, Charles	725
Sterry, Edward	5,850
Sterry, Sally M	500
Stetson, Calvin R	1,500
Stevens, Mrs. Elizabeth	350
Stevens, Henry E	——
St. Mary's Church	2,000
St. Patrick's Church	7,000
Stewart, Catharine	750
Stoddard, Isaac N	540
Stoddard, Romain	1,350
Storer, Egbert	7,075
Story, James A, est	2,575
Story, J. Palmer	650
Story, Nathan B	384
Story, Phebe E., Mrs	3,975
Story, Samuel, heirs	1,900
Stott, John	7,750
Stott, Joseph	1,200
Strong, Asa	3,830
Stuart, Frank S	1,850
Sturm, Max	700
Stocker, Catharine, Mrs	250
Stockwell, Lone E	300
Startevant, Albert P	53,050
Stutson, William P	100
Subert, Sylvester	6,485
Sullivan, Andrew J	165
Sullivan, Daniel	740
Sullivan, Daniel, 2d	1,800
Sullivan, Daniel & Mary Kelly	1,200
Sullivan, Eugene L	200
Sullivan, Jeremiah	1,500
Sullivan, John	500
Sullivan, John and Catharine	1,350
Sullivan, John T	1,400
Sullivan, Marty	1,500
Sullivan, Owen	1,000
Sullivan, Patrick	240
Sutherland, Joseph	220
Sutliffe, Mrs. J. Amelia	3,100
Swan, Lucius C	8,138
Swan, Sanford B	800
Sweeney, Patrick	1,200
Sweet, George C	1,400
Sydleman, Harriet R	2,700
Symonds, George	1,250

Name	Amount
Taft, Erauder	1,775
Tanner, Gilbert H	4,010
Tarbox, Mary E	1,300
Tarrant, Nicholas	1,125
Taylor, Cebra L., Mrs	1,150
Taylor, Ellis	2,300
Tefft, Villara A	1,000
Tefft, William	2,908

Tenney, Allen ... 4,750
Thames Iron Works ... 25,000
Thames National Bank ... 7,500
Thatcher, Betsey & Frances ... 720
Thayer, John R ... 165
Theis, Susan G ... 330
Thomas, Amelia M ... 800
Thomas, Caroline L ... 5,545
Thomas, Caroline L., trustee ... 6,000
Thomas, Mrs. E. Y ... 2,950
Thomas, Henry, est ... 7,000
Thompson, Charles ... 2,490
Thompson, Edward R ... 1,015
Thresher, Mrs. Annie H ... 3,420
Thresher, Seneca S ... 3,610
Thurston, Elizabeth M ... 600
Thurston, Laura S ... 6,150
Thute, Patrick H ... 700
Tibbetts, Henry W ... 60
Tillinghast, Francis A ... 4,020
Tillinghast, Lewis A ... 165
Tilton, Benjamin ... 1,200
Tingley, Mrs. Sarah E ... 8,200
Taft, David ... 800
Tompkins, Benjamin W ... 29,835
Tompkins, Lorenzo D ... 204
Toomey, David ... 1,500
Toomey, John ... 2,700
Toomey, Patrick ... 600
Torbush, Henry ... 2,300
Torrance, Archibald ... 1,200
Totoket Mills ... 102,000
Tourtelotte, Charles P ... 1,000
Tourtelotte, Isaac N., est ... 500
Tourtelotte, James N ... 2,350
Tourtelotte, Mrs. William B ... 500
Towne, William H ... 1,500
Tracy, Charles M ... 650
Tracy, Edwin A ... 2,525
Tracy, Elijah ... 2,900
Tracy, Timothy W ... 950
Tratton, Charles H ... 500
Treadway, Frederick W ... 10,600
Treadway, F. W., trustee ... 5,270
Treadway, John F ... 850
Treadway, Martha ... 200
Tree, Daniel ... 800
Tree, Sarah E ... 900
Tribey, John, est ... 1,875
Trinity Church Parish ... 1,200
Troland, Archibald ... 4,878
Troland, James ... 1,700
Troland, John ... 2,750
Trowbridge, Willard ... 5,380
True, William D ... 1,525
Trueman, John H ... 4,100
Trueman, Joseph B ... 15,600
Trumbull, Mrs A. N ... 3,000
Trumbull, D. L., est ... 500
Trumbull, Jonathan ... 7,580
Tubbs, Abagail C ... 1,000
Tubbs, Charles W. L ... 2,000
Tubbs, Oliver H ... 300
Tubbs, William ... 9,795
Tucker, Dennison B., est ... 4,500
Tucker, William C ... 290
Tufts, Charles F ... 925
Tufts, William F ... 940
Turner, Edward L ... 2,700
Turner, Belle B ... 2,300
Turner, Isaac ... 1,475
Turner, Maria T ... 13,000
Turner, Sidney ... 13,130
Tweedy, Mrs. Harriet N ... 7,800
Tweedy & Gray ... 3,050
Tyler, Frank and Elizabeth ... 6,995
Tyler, O. S., est ... 2,115

Uncas Hall Co ... 14,000
Uncas National Bank ... 4,000
Universalist Society ... 1,200
Upham, Ellen G ... 2,000
Underwood, Thomas H ... 1,400
Utley, Frank ... 700
Utley, John C., est ... 2,000

Vallett, Jeremiah ... 300
Van Cott, Mrs. Sarah P ... 1,800
Vaughn, Alfred H ... 16,400
Vergason, Calvin ... 845
Vergason, Daniel B ... 455
Vergason, James H ... 165

Name	Amount
Vergason, James H	$ 165
Vergason, Fremont	150
Vergason, Nelson	6,891
Vergason, William	1,175
Vickers, Laura W.	2,200
Victor Heating Co.	6,000
Volkmar, Justus	200
Voorhees, Elias.	650
Voorhees, Thomas	800
Wade, Jared	96
Wade, John L.	1,500
Wait, John T.	23,000
Wait, John T. & J. Trumbull	1,500
Wait, Joseph J	315
Wakefield, Clovis W	1,500
Walker, Dennis T.	2,100
Walker, Hill & Edgarton	960
Walker, James.	5,000
Walker, Julia F.	2,000
Wallace, Samuel R	480
Walls, Hardin	440
Walsh, John.	1,900
Walsh, William.	7,800
Ward, Nannie B	1,800
Ward, Nancy H. est., and Mary B.	1,500
Ward, Patrick	1,600
Ward, William D	3.733
Warner, John E	300
Warren, George W.	2,575
Washburn, Edward T.	2,500
Wasley, Fred. R	5,150
Waterman, David H	2,335
Waters, Charlotte.	1,000
Waters, George.	480
Waters, Jerusha	480
Watson, Mrs. Myra	240
Watt, James.	1,050
Wattles, Oliver P.	15,420
Webb, Charles.	8,100
Webb, Charles, guardian	2,200
Webb, Charles, guardian	2,100
Webb, Charles, trustee.	13,800
Webb, John B	2,700
Webb, Lillie M	2,170
Webb, Julius.	32,750
Webb, Richard H.	720

Name	Amount
Webster, Claudius R.	$1,650
Webster, Edward Z.	5,500
Weitzel, Charles F	330
Welch, Albert E	1,200
Welch, Emma and Emily	900
Welch, Gamaliel M	1,350
Welch, John.	1,000
Welch & Moshier.	1,000
Welch, William	1,000
Welden, Albert R.	1,100
Welden, Patrick	1.320
Welden, Stark & Gallaher	11,550
Weller, John	2,175
Wells, David A	25,930
Wells, F. A	5,025
Wells, F. A. & Co.	6,000
West, True	330
West, William.	400
Weir, Eliza G	2,420
Whaley Brothers	
Whaley, Charles H	480
Whaley, Frances E.	2,250
Whaley, Levi G......t	2,610
Whaley, Stephen F	1,775
Whaley, William E	—
Wheeler, Avery D.	3,000
Wheeler, Amos T.	220
Wheeler, Charles H	200
Wheeler, Emma L.	2,500
Wheeler, George W.	1,830
Whittaker, Horace	12,015
Whittaker, John.	1,200
White, John	1,400
Whiteley, Mrs. George	2,200
Whiting, Celia E.	2.170
Whitney, Samuel A.	2,625
Whittemore, M. Maturin	2.575
Wicker, Henry	300
Wightman, George P	2,300
Wightman, Wolcott C.	2,200
Wilbur, Mrs. Asenath	1,100
Wilbur, Mrs. Jeremiah.	320
Wilbur, John, est	1,500
Wilbur, Labra A	1,100
Wilcox, Asher H	2,100
Wilcox, Gordon	1,500
Wilcox, Mrs. Mary	2,702

Wilcox, William B.... ....$8,370
Wilkinson, Jared P., est.............1,200
Willard, John...... 8,025
Willey, Edward G...................1,900
Williams, Abby C., and Rebecca.....6,900
Williams, Charles M...............1,500
Williams, Elisha, est...............1,500
Williams, E. Winslow.............46,845
Williams, Erasmus J............... 360
Williams, George E................1,500
Williams, Henry...................2,800
Williams, Lucretia.................. 180
Williams, Mary A..................2,412
Williams, Roger S.................. 125
Williams, William M...............7,150
Willis, Calvin G...................1,400
Willoughby, Archa P...............7,515
Wilsky, Herman....................1,040
Wilson, Andrew.................... 800
Wilson, Thomas....................2,440
Winchester, Mrs. James............1,500
Winship, Horace B.................. 500
Winship, Joseph F..................1,000
Winship, T. Y......................11,635
Winters, Chas. J....................7,950
Winters, Swift & Co................4,700
Witter, Hattie L.................... 660
Witter, William.....................2,950
Wolfarth, Charles...................1,900
Wolfarth, John......................1,440
Wolfe, Conrad.......................1,300
Wolfe, Martin.......................4,500
Wood, Willet R., est..............16,975
Woodhull, Elizabeth B.............8,000
Woodmansey, Charles S............1,050
Woodruff, James H.................1,400
Woodward, Calvin H............... 300
Woodward, Daniel, est............5,000
Woodward, H. R.................. 300
Woodward, Jane G................ 516
Woodward, R. G....................2,625
Woodworth, Elias...................3,312
Woodworth, Thomas B.............8,375
Woodworth & Small................1,200
Worden, Mrs. Ann.................1,800
Worth, J. C........................$ 230
Worth, J. C & Co...................1,315
Worthington, Eliza.................1,800
Wyman, Alfred E.................. 100

Yantic Store Co.....................2,625
Yantic Woolen Co.................111,825
Yeomans, George L................1,465
Yerrington, Ezra W................3,825
Yerrington, Stephen N............16,690
Young, A. A. & F. Johnson, trustees..4,000
Young, Charles....................36,766
Young, David.......................4,125
Young, Frances E.................. 900
Young, Mrs. E. A...................3,100
Young, George......................2,500
Young, Mary E......................1,500
Young, Sarah B.................... 100
Young, William B..................1,525

Zimmerman, George............... 800

NON-RESIDENTS.

Adams Express Co................ 1,125
Alden, James C.....................4,500
Alger, Marie Louise................5,500
Albertine, Mrs. Ann................1,625
Armstrong, Eliza, heirs............2,100
Arnold, Rouse H.................. 450

Babcock, Clarence W.............. 300
Bailey, Charles H.................12,000
Baurgua, Peter......................1,500
Bentley, Edwin.....................4,500
Bentley, George R..................5,800
Berry, Elmore H....................1,000
Bill, Ledyard.......................2,400
Billings, Samuel D..................1,000
Bingham, Ellen F...................1,200
Bingham, George, heirs........... 400
Birkery, Cornelius................. 800

Name	Amount
Bishop, N. P.	$1,500
Boozang, James F.	900
Boone, Mary P	1,500
Bradley, Henry E.	1,200
Brewster, Albert G.	1,000
Brewster, John	300
Brockway, E. D	3,200
Brown, John	9,500
Brown, Michael	300
Buckholly, John B.	100
Burdick, John	400
Burdick, William	3,000
Buell, Julius	6,010
Buell, Rachel S	1,600
Burnham, Andrew C	1,500
Butler, John	1,000
Callaghan, William, heirs	12,000
Carroll, George	300
Carroll, Michael	100
Carter, Charles W	5,000
Champlin, Edmund L	3,800
Chappell, A. H	2,000
Charlton, Charles H	900
Childs, Mary E	6,000
Church, Andrew J	2,500
Clark, Joseph F. S	3,000
Clark, Susan	300
Coit, Daniel, est	9,800
Cooley, John G	1,500
Cox, George H	150
Coyle, John	1,000
Coyle, John B	4,050
Craven, James	3,000
Dawson, James	5,175
De Bruycker, F	1,750
Denison, John L., trustee	4,500
Downer, Ellen	150
Doyle, John B.	9,000
Doyle, Thomas	1,000
Driscoll, Timothy	700
Durfey, Joseph P	1,500
Durfey, Edward	2,100
Durfey, C. A	700
Edwards, Peleg	$ 300
Fanning, John T	600
Farnum, Mary A., and Amelia L.	7,000
Farnum, Sarah A	7,200
Farrington, Martin L	300
Fillmore, Ann M	1,000
Fitch, William H.	850
Fitch, W. H., trustee	2,800
Fornier, Theodore	150
Forsyth, James F., est	1,500
Fox, John, guardian	1,000
Freeman, George, heirs	600
Fuller, Henry A	8,500
Fuller, Reuben B	200
Fuller, Robert B	1,200
Gallup, David, est	3,500
Gallup, Emily C	4,500
Gallup, John M	1,800
Gardner, Elisha M	3,000
Gaylord, Charles H	24,000
Geer, Oliver J	900
Geer, Nathan	500
Gifford, Mrs. Gurdon	1,100
Gladding, Charles F	1,400
Gillogly, Mrs. James P.	800
Gleason, Harriet N	1,700
Goddard, Mary N	6,000
Godfrey, Jonathan	3,000
Goodrich, Emma	3,000
Goodrich, Nelson	3,300
Griswold, Abel G	1,000
Guine, Jane	100
Hammond, Hannah	5,000
Hare, John T	50
Harrington, Mrs. A. L	4,000
Harvey, Ira W	9,000
Harris, Sybil A	1,000
Hart, Leo	2,800
Hawkins, John C	2,800

Hatch & Foote ... $ 500
Hazen, George W ... 2,300
Hedge, Charles D ... 3,000
Hewitt, John F ... 1,600
Hillhouse, David ... 1,800
Higgins, John ... 100
Hogan, James ... 300
Holmes, Joseph ... 3,500
Hoxie, Albert F ... 450
Huntington, Miss Emily ... 2,500
Hyde, Fred G ... 1,500

Jillson, Lucy M ... 1,700
Johnson, William G ... 3,300
Jones, Patrick ... 1,700

Kane, James H., children of ... 400
Kelley, Patrick ... 3,400
Kibbe, John M ... 1,200
Kimball, Lucy M ... 4,000
Kimball, William, heirs ... 1,500
King, Felix ... 3,300
Kingsley, J. P ... 5,000
Kingsley, Milton and Walter ... 3,200
Kinney, Henry M ... 100
Kinney, Joseph ... 3,300
Kinney, Joseph, 2d ... 1,800
Kirker, James ... 5,500

Ladd, Marvin ... 3,300
Lamb, Winslow M ... 3,800
Lamman, David T., est ... 4,500
Lathrop, Don F., heirs ... 2,200
Leach, Eunice E ... 1,200
Leffingwell, John ... 2,350
Lewis, Allen C., est ... 4,500
Lord, Mrs. Simeon ... 450
Lucas, Samuel ... 1,925
Luce, Mrs. Edward ... 3,000
Lusk, Elizabeth ... 5,250
Luther, Linus A ... 300

Manwaring, James H ... 600
Maples, Annie H. B ... 11,000
Marcus, Jacob ... $ 400
Martin, Julia A., est ... 1,600
Marshall, John ... 700
Marx, Samuel E ... 700
Mayer, David ... 2,800
McCoy, Thos ... 900
McIntyre, Mary and others ... 800
McDougald, Mrs. H W ... 3,500
Metzger, Andrew ... 700
Miner, James C ... 1,000
Moriarty, Mary ... 2,850
Mosier, Mabel W ... 2,250
Murphy, Patrick D ... 1,300
Murphy, Richard ... 400
Murtagh, Thomas R ... 800
Myene, Joseph ... 500
Myene, Peter ... 200

New London Northern R. R. Co ... 8,900
Newell, Lydia E ... 1,300
Noble, Charles ... 900
Norton, Horace W ... 2,000

Owens & Mercer ... 400

Page, John B ... 1,500
Palmer, Charles T ... 4,000
Palmer, Jonathan J ... 1,700
Park, Delano J ... 1,000
Park, Thos. H ... 2,200
Parker, Timothy & Wm. B ... 300
Peck, John and John D. Sullivan ... 2,200
Piatt, Julia G ... 800
Pitt, Eagles & Johnson ... 6,500
Plumacr, George L ... 4,500
Post, John ... 400
Pratt, Amasa ... 500

Reagan, Timothy ... 1,000
Reynolds, Job ... 4,200
Riley, Patrick ... 1,500
Ripley, Daniel C ... 2,000
Richardson, Ann M ... 1,700

Ripley, George C $1,000
Robbins, William N 150
Robertson, John 1,500
Rogers, Josephine 100
Rogers, Samuel L 550
Rudd, Jane L 2,000

Saunders, Horace N 200
Sawin, John W 1,100
Shay, John C 550
Sharron, Ezra 150
Smith, Mrs. Horace 2,300
Smith, William H 1,600
Spellman, Nicholas D 2,500
Spellman, William 600
Spencer, Jane L 1,500
Spencer, John J 250
Staples, Caroline T 300
Stanton, Rowland 6,000
Starkweather, H. H., heirs 3,000
Sterry, F. W 600
Sterry, J. A. & A. P. McGrath 6,000
Stewart, Calvin M 2,250
Stiles, Ezra 3,000
Stodder, Charles B 2,800
Sullivan, James 75
Sullivan, Jeremiah 825
Sullivan, Timothy 250
Swift, Edwin B 1,700
Talbot, Almira B 1,100
Talcott, Charles H 1,800
Tanner, Asahel 4,000
Thompson, William H 150
Thornhill, William H 200
Tiffany, Adelaide H 1,500
Tinkham, William 30,000
Tyler, Huldah and Josephine 3,000
Ward, Horatio N 100
Wellington, T. W. & Co 3,000
Welles, Mrs. Gideon, and Alice N. Gilbert 2,500
Wetmore, Thomas T 1,200
White, Elizabeth M 31,250
Whittlesey, John 1,000
Whittier, R. H. and H. L. Greene $3,500
Williams, Charles Augustus 10,000
Williams, Jerome W 4,000
Wilson, Alfred J 300
Weissard, John C 100
Wright, Jeremiah 200
Worcester Coal Co 4,000

PENSION EXEMPTS.

Appleton, Henry P 1,000
Bentley, Mrs. Mary 1,000
Brown, Reuben B 1,000
Corey, Andrew E 1,000
Carleton, Charles M 1,000
Carpenter, Delano M 1,000
Caruthers, William H 3,000
Carroll, Charles H 800
Carroll, George, non-resident 1,000
Chapman, Mrs. Giles 600
Clark, Jeanette 1,000
Connors, James 1,000
Corcoran, Stephen 1,000
Denison, John J 900
Driscoll, Michael 600
Enos, John J 960
Farrell, Thos 1,000
Filburn, Mary 1,000
Gleason, Ann M 700
Hill, John L 1,000
Howe, S. G. & W. R 1,000
Kelly, John 1,000
Kelly, Michael 700
Kelly, Michael 720
Keppler, Sebastian P 1,000
Kimball, James 1,000
Kinney, Albert B 180
McMahon, Gilbert 950
Moore, Michael 752
O'Kelley, John 1,000
Phinney, Elisha 1,000
Rogers, Joab B 1,000
Shaw, Daniel B 1,000
Stanley, James 1,000
Strickland, James M 150

Sullivan, Patrick O.	$ 900
Wallen, George L.	550
Weiler, John	330
Wilbur, John A	1,710
Williams, Calvin	900
Wilson, Joseph	360
Wise, William H	600
Wood, Ira I	900
Woodward, Calvin H	1,000
Zimmerman, George	1,000

EXEMPT PROPERTY.

New London County	30,000
New London Co. Agricultural Soc	8,000
New London Co. M. Ins. Co.	5,850
Norwich, Town of	180,800
Norwich, City of	203,000
Norwich, First Eccles. Society of	33,664
Norwich, Second Eccles. Society of	35,000
Norwich, Fourth Eccles. Society of	15,000
Norwich, Broadway Eccles. Soc. of	45,000
Norwich, Park Eccles. Society of	100,000
Norwich, Free Academy	123,500
Norwich Central School District	140,000
Norwich, West Chelsea School Dist	55,000
Norwich, Town Street School Dist	15,000
Norwich, Town Street School Dist	75,000
Norwich, N. Bank	6,000
Thames Bank	15,000
Merchants N. Bank	6,000
Uncas N. Bank	8,000
Shetucket N. Bank	10,610
Second National Bank	8,900
Norwich Savings Society	7,847,930
Chelsea Savings Bank	3,433,735
Dime Savings Bank	1,258,424
Norwich Mutual Ins. Co.	6,840
Norwich and Worcester R. R. Co	200,000
Central Methodist Church	15,500
East Main Street Methodist Church	5,000
Sachem Street Methodist Church	8,000
Bean Hill Methodist Church	5,000
Greeneville Methodist Church	5,000
Mount Calvary Baptist Church	3,500
First Baptist Church	17,300
Greeneville Baptist Church	8,000
Central Baptist Church	$20,000
Christ Episcopal Church	55,000
Trinity Episcopal Church	25,000
Universalist Caurch	15,000
St. Mary's R. C. Church	24,000
St Patrick's R. C. Church	226,000
Taftville R. C. Church	10,000
Occum R. C. Church	7,000
German Lutheran Church	6,000
African Colored Church	2,000
New London Northern R. R. Co	10,000
Eliza Huntington Memorial Home	68,300
Otis Library Association	10,000
Children's Home	7,000
Sheltering Arms	4,000
Cemeteries	50,000

Total List of Residents	$12,543,877
Total List of Non-Residents	613,860
	$13,157,737
Total value of property	$27,672,252

Total List Pension Exempt Property	$ 41,602
Total List Exempt Property	14,472,913
	$14,514,515

ADDITIONS BY BOARD OF RELIEF.

Adams, John T., est	750
Coscoran, James	150
Doolittle, Dwight	200
Dunn, William H	100
Flynn, Patrick	525
Fuller, Theodore	750
Fuller, John	200
Gardner, Harriet M	5,000
Gordon, Charles M	150
Heebner, Henry	100
Harvey, Irving & Co	1,065
Murphy, John, Occum	100
Plunkett, Thomas	150
Whaley, Wm. E	6,750

GRAND LIST OF NORWICH FROM 1800 TO THE PRESENT TIME.

Year	Amount	Year	Amount
1800	$1,797,879	1863	$ 9,816,565
1810	2,231,710	1864	10,494,035
1820	2,048,366	1865	10,970,435
1830	2,155,133	1866	11,877,860
1835	7,551,795	1867	13,143,467
1840	4,844,017	1868	13,210,202
1845	3,943,623	1869	13,509,561
1850	4,446,480	1870	14,431,194
1851	4,889,124	1871	14,799,422
1852	5,158,660	1872	15,544,119
1853	6,583,687	1873	15,339,071
1854	6,913,908	1874	15,199,672
1855	6,876,713	1875	14,732,840
1856	7,080,653	1876	14,602,901
1857	6,829,778	1877	13,801,789
1858	6,884,722	1878	13,431,430
1859	7,592,651	1879	13,349,295
1860	8,000,521	1880	13,160,572
1861	9,151,417	1881	13,119,742
1862	8,926,028	1882	13,036,973

UNITED STATES GOVERNMENT.

JANUARY 1ST, 1884.

	SALARY.
President of the United States—Chester A. Arthur, of New York	$50,000
Fred. J. Phillips, Private Secretary.	
O. L. Pruden, Assistant Private Secretary.	
Clayton McMichael, United States Marshal, District of Columbia.	
Vice-President (by election as President pro tem. of the Senate)—George F. Edmunds, of Vermont	8,000

DEPARTMENT OF STATE.

Secretary of State—F. T. Frelinghuysen, of New Jersey	$8,000
Assistant Secretary—Vacant	3,500
Second Assistant Secretary—William Hunter	3,500
Third Assistant Secretary—John Davis	3,500
Chief Clerk—Sevello A. Brown	2,500

DEPARTMENT OF THE TREASURY.

Secretary of the Treasury—Charles J. Folger, of New York	$8,000
Assistant Secretary—John C. New	4,500
Assistant Secretary—Henry F. French	4,500
Chief Clerk—Amos Webster	3,000
Supervising Architect—M. E. Bell	4,500
Director of the Mint—H. R. Burchard	4,500
Chief of the Bureau of Engraving and Printing—Truman M. Burrill	4,500
First Comptroller—William Lawrence	5,000
Commissioner of Customs—Henry C. Johnson	4,000
Register of the Treasury—Blanch K. Bruce	4,000
Treasurer of the United States—A. U. Wyman	6,000
Comptroller of the Currency—John Jay Knox	3,000

Commissioner of Internal Revenue—Walter Evans ..... $ 6,000
Superintendent United States Coast Survey—Julius E. Hilgard 4,500
Chief of Bureau of Statistics—Joseph Nimmo, Jr.
Chief of Appointment Division—J. B. Butler.
General Superintendent Life-Saving Service—Sumner I. Kimball.

DEPARTMENT OF WAR.

Secretary of War—Robert T. Lincoln, of Illinois $8,000
Chief Clerk—John Tweedale 2,500
Quartermaster-General—Brevet Major-General Samuel B. Holabird.
Commissary-General—Brigadier-General Robert Macfeely.
Surgeon-General—Vacant.
Paymaster-General—Brigadier-General W. B. Rochester.
Chief of Engineers—Brevet Major-General Horatio G. Wright.
Chief of Ordinance—Brigadier-General Stephen V. Benet.
Judge-Advocate-General—Brigadier-General D. G. Swaim.
Chief of Signal Corps—Brevet Major-General William B. Hazen.

HEADQUARTERS OF THE ARMY.

Lieutenant-General of the Army—P. H. Sheridan.
Adjutant-General—Brigadier-General Richard C. Drum.
Inspector-General—Brevet Major-General D. B. Sacket.

DEPARTMENT OF THE NAVY.

Secretary of the Navy—William E. Chandler, of New Hampshire .. $8,000
Chief Clerk—John W. Hogg 2,520
Chief of Bureau of Yards and Docks—Rear Admiral Edward T. Nichols.
Chief of Bureau of Navigation—Captain John G. Walker.
Chief of Bureau of Ordinance—Captain Montgomery Sicard.
Chief of Bureau of Provisions and Clothing—Paymaster-Gen. Joseph A. Smith.
Chief of Bureau of Medicine and Surgery—Surgeon-General Ph. S. Wales.
Chief of Bureau of Construction and Repair—Chief Constructor Theodore G. Wilson.
Chief of Bureau of Equipment and Recruiting—Commodore Earl English.
Chief of Bureau of Steam Engineering—Vacant.
Admiral of the Navy—D. D. Porter.
Vice-Admiral—S. C. Rowan, Governor Naval Asylum, Philadelphia.
Pay Inspector—Richard Washington.
Commandant of Marine Corps—Colonel C. G. MacCawley.
Superintendent of U. S. Naval Observatory—Rear Admiral R. W. Shufeldt.
Chief Hydrographer—Commander J. R. Bartlett.
Superintendent Naval Academy—Captain F. M. Ramsay.

POST OFFICE DEPARTMENT.

Postmaster-General—W. Q. Gresham, of Indiana	$8,000
Chief Clerk—Geo. H. Walker	2,200
First Assistant Postmaster-General—Frank Hatton	4,000
Second Assistant Postmaster-General—Richard A. Elmer	4,000
Third Assistant Postmaster-General—A. D. Hazen	4,000
Superintendent of Foreign Mail Service—Vacant	3,000
Superintendent of Money Order System—Charles F. MacDonald	3,000

DEPARTMENT OF THE INTERIOR.

Secretary of the Interior—Henry M. Teller, of Colorado	$8,000
Assistant Secretary—Merritt L. Joslyn	3,500
Chief Clerk—George M. Lockwood	2,750
Commissioner of Land Office—N. C. MacFarland	4,000
Commissioner of Pensions—Wm. W. Dudley	5,000
Commissioner of Patents—Benj. H. Butterworth	4,500
Indian Commissioner—Hiram Price	4,000
Superintendent of Census—C. W. Seaton	5,000
Commissioner of Education—John Eaton	3,000

DEPARTMENT OF JUSTICE.

Attorney-General—B. H. Brewster, of Pennsylvania	$8,000
Solicitor-General—Samuel F. Phillips	7,000
Assistant Attorney-General—Wm. A. Maury	5,000
Assistant Attorney-General—Thomas Simons	5,000
Assistant Attorney-General, Department of the Interior—Jos. K. McCammon	5,000
Assistant Attorney-General, Post-Office Department—A. A. Freeman	5,000
Examiner of Claims, State Department—Henry O'Connor.	
Chief Clerk—Jas. Rankin Young.	
Solicitor of the Treasury—Kenneth Rayner.	

DEPARTMENT OF AGRICULTURE.

Commissioner of Agriculture—George B. Loring, of Massachusetts $3,000

Chief Clerk—E. A. Carman.	Botanist—Dr. George Vasey.
Statistician—J. R. Dodge.	Chemist—Peter Collier.
Entomologist—C. V. Riley.	Microscopist—Thomas Taylor.

JUDICIARY.

SUPREME COURT OF THE UNITED STATES.

Chief Justice—Morrison R. Waite, of Ohio $10,500

Justice Samuel F. Miller, of Iowa	$10,000	Justice Wm. B. Woods, of Georgia	$10,000
Justice Stephen J. Field, of Cal.	10,000	Justice Stanley Matthews, of Ohio	10,000
Justice Joseph P. Bradley, of N. J.	10,000	Justice Horace Gray, of Mass.	10,000
Justice John H. Harlan, of Ky.	10,000	Justice Sam'l Blatchford, of N. Y.	10,000

Reporter .... J. C. Bancroft Davis.

Clerk .... J. H. McKenney.

CIRCUIT COURTS OF THE UNITED STATES.

First Judicial Circuit—Justice Horace Gray, of Massachusetts. Districts of Maine, New Hampshire, Massachusetts and Rhode Island.
Circuit Judge—John Lowell, Boston, Mass. Salary, $6,000.

Second Judicial Circuit—Justice Samuel Blatchford, of New York. Districts of Vermont, Connecticut, Northern New York, Southern New York and Eastern New York.
Circuit Judge—William J. Wallace, of New York. Salary, $6,000.

Third Judicial Circuit—Justice Joseph P. Bradley, of New Jersey. Districts of New Jersey, Eastern Pennsylvania, Western Pennsylvania and Delaware.
Circuit Judge—William McKennan, of Pennsylvania. Salary, $6,000.

Fourth Judicial Circuit—Chief Justice Morrison R. Waite, of Ohio. Districts of Maryland, West Virginia, Virginia, North Carolina and South Carolina.
Circuit Judge—Hugh L. Bond, of Maryland. Salary, $6,000.

Fifth Judicial Circuit—Justice William B. Woods, of Georgia. Districts of Georgia, Northern Florida, Southern Florida, Northern Alabama, Southern Alabama, Mississippi, Louisiana, Eastern Texas and Western Texas.
Circuit Judge—Don A. Pardee, of Louisiana. Salary, $6,000.

Sixth Judicial Circuit—Justice Stanley Matthews, of Ohio. Districts of Northern Ohio, Southern Ohio, Eastern Michigan, Western Michigan, Kentucky, Eastern Tennessee and Western Tennessee.
Circuit Judge—John Baxter, of Knoxville, Tenn. Salary, $6,000.

Seventh Judicial Circuit—Justice John M. Harlan, of Kentucky. Districts of Indiana, Northern Illinois, Southern Illinois and Wisconsin.
Circuit Judge—Thomas Drummond, of Chicago, Ill. Salary, $6,000.

Eighth Judicial Circuit—Justice Samuel F. Miller, of Keokuk, Iowa. Districts of Minnesota, Iowa, Eastern Missouri, Western Missouri, Kansas, Eastern Arkansas, Western Arkansas and Nebraska.
Circuit Judge—Geo. W. McCrary, of Keokuk. Salary, $6,000.

Ninth Judicial Circuit—Justice Stephen J. Field, of San Francisco, California. Districts of California, Oregon and Nevada.
Circuit Judge—Lorenzo Sawyer, San Francisco, California. Salary, $6,000.

DISTRICT JUDGES.

Alabama (N. M. & Ss.)—John Bruce, Montgomery, Fifth Circuit, $3,500.
Arkansas (E. D.)—Henry C. Caldwell, Little Rock, Eighth Circuit, $3,500.
Arkansas (W. D.)—Isaac C. Parker, Fort Smith, Eighth Circuit, $3,500.
California—Ogden Hoffman, San Francisco, Ninth Circuit, $5,000.
Colorado—Moses Hallet, Denver, Eighth Circuit, $5,000.
Connecticut—Nathaniel Shipman, Hartford, Second Circuit, $3,500.
Delaware—Edward C. Bradford, Wilmington, Third Circuit, $3,500.
Florida (N. D.)—Thomas Settle, Jacksonville, Fifth Circuit, $3,500.
Florida (S. D.)—James W. Locke, Key West, Fifth Circuit, $3,500.

GEORGIA—Henry K. McCoy, Atlanta, Fifth Circuit, $3,500.
GEORGIA (S. D.)—John Erskine, Savannah, $3,500.
ILLINOIS (N. D.)—Henry W. Blodgett, Chicago, Seventh Circuit, $3,500.
ILLINOIS (S. D.)—Samuel H. Treat, Springfield, Seventh Circuit, $3,500.
INDIANA—William S. Woods, Indianapolis, Seventh Circuit, $3,500.
IOWA (N. D.)—Oliver P. Shiras, Dubuque, $3,500.
IOWA (S. D.)—James M. Love, Keokuk, Eighth Circuit, $3,500.
KANSAS—Cassius G. Foster, Topeka, Eighth Circuit, $3,500.
KENTUCKY—John W. Barr, Louisville, Sixth Circuit, $3,500.
LOUISIANA (E. D.)—Edward C. Billings, New Orleans, Fifth Circuit, $4,500.
LOUISIANA (W. D.)—Alex. Boarman.
MAINE—Nathan Webb, Portland, First Circuit, $3,500.
MARYLAND—Thos. J. Morris, Baltimore, Fourth Circuit, $4,000.
MASSACHUSETTS—Thos. L. Nelson, Boston, First Circuit, $4,000.
MICHIGAN (E. D.)—Henry B. Brown, Detroit, Sixth Circuit, $3,500.
MICHIGAN (W. D.)—Solomon L. Withey, Grand Rapids, Sixth Circuit, $3,500.
MINNESOTA—Rensselaer R. Nelson, St. Paul, Eighth Circuit, $3,500.
MISSISSIPPI (N. & S. Dist.)—Robert Andrew Hill, Oxford, Fifth Circuit, $3,500.
MISSOURI (E. D.)—Samuel Treat, St. Louis, Eighth Circuit, $3,500.
MISSOURI (W. D.)—Arnold Krekel, Jefferson City, Eighth Circuit, $3,500.
NEBRASKA—Elmer S. Dundy, Falls City, Eighth Circuit, $3,500.
NEVADA—Geo. M. Sabin, Carson, Ninth Circuit, $3,500.
NEW HAMPSHIRE—Daniel Clark, Manchester, First Circuit, $3,500.
NEW JERSEY—John T. Nixon, Trenton, Third Circuit, $4,000.
NEW YORK (N. D.)—Alfred C. Coxe, Syracuse, Second Circuit, $4,000.
NEW YORK (S. D.)—Addison Brown, New York City, Second Circuit, $4,000.
NEW YORK (E. D.)—Charles L. Benedict, Brooklyn, Second Circuit, $4,000.
NORTH CAROLINA (E. D.)—Augustus S. Seymour, Elizabeth City, Fourth Circuit, $3,500.
NORTH CAROLINA (W. D.)—Robert P. Dick, Greensboro, Fourth Circuit, $3,500.
OHIO (N. D.)—Martin Welker, Wooster, Sixth Circuit, $3,500.
OHIO (S. D.)—George R. Sage, Cincinnati, Sixth Circuit, $4,000.
OREGON—Matthew P. Deady, Portland, Ninth Circuit, $3,500.
PENNSYLVANIA (E. D.)—William Butler, Philadelphia, Third Circuit, $4,000.
PENNSYLVANIA (W. D.)—Marcus W. Acheson, Pittsburg, Third Circuit, $4,000.
RHODE ISLAND—L. Barron B. Colt, Bristol, First Circuit, $3,500.
SOUTH CAROLINA—George S. Bryan, Charleston, Fourth Circuit, $3,500.
TENNESSEE (E. D.)—David M. Key, Chattanooga, Sixth Circuit, $3,500.
TENNESSEE (M. D.)—David M. Key.
TENNESSEE (W. D.)—Eli Shelby Hammond, Memphis, $3,500.
TEXAS (E. D.)—Amos Morrill, Galveston, Fifth Circuit, $3,500.
TEXAS (W. D.)—Ezekiel B. Turner, Austin, Fifth Circuit, $3,500.
TEXAS (N. D.)—A. P. McCormick, Dallas, Fifth Circuit, $3,500.
VERMONT—Hoyt H. Wheeler, Jamaica, Second Circuit, $3,500.
VIRGINIA (E. D.)—Robert W. Hughes, Norfolk, Fourth Circuit, $3,500.
VIRGINIA (W. D.)—John Paul, Harrisburg, Fourth Circuit, $3,500.
WEST VIRGINIA—John J. Jackson, Jr., Parkersburg, Fourth Circuit, $3,500.
WISCONSIN (E. D.)—Charles E. Dyer, Racine, Seventh Circuit, $3,500.
WISCONSIN (W. D.)—Romanzo Bunn, Madison, Seventh Circuit, $3,500.

UNITED STATES COURT OF CLAIMS.

Chief Justice Charles D. Drake.

Vacant.

Judge Charles C. Nott.

Judge William A. Richardson.

Judge Glenni W. Scofield.

Chief Clerk—Archibald Hopkins.

DISTRICT OF COLUMBIA.

Supreme Court.

Chief Justice—D. K. Cartter, $4,500.

Associate Justices.

Andrew Wylie, $4,000.

Arthur McArthur, $4,000.

A. B. Wagner, $4,000.

W. S. Cox, $4,000.

C. P. James, $4,000.

Chief Clerk—R. J. Meigs.

SUPREME COURTS IN THE TERRITORIES.

ARIZONA:	RESIDENCE.	SALARY.
Chief Justice.		
Chas. G. W. French	Prescott	$3,000
Associate Justices.		
1. D. H. Pinney	Phœnix	3,000
2. H. W. Shelden	Tucson	3,000

DAKOTA:		
Chief Justice.		
Alonzo J. Edgerton	Yankton	3,000
Associate Justices.		
1. Sanford A. Hudson	Fargo	3,000
2. Wm. E. Church	Deadwood	3,000
3. Vacant		3,000

IDAHO:—		
Chief Justice.		
John T. Morgan	Oxford	3,000
Associate Justices.		
1. Norman Buck	Lewiston	3,000
2. Henry E. Prickett	Boise City	3,000

MONTANA:		
Chief Justice.		
Decius S. Wade	Helena	3,000
Associate Justices.		
1. Wm. J. Galbraith	Virginia City	3,000
2. Vacant.		

NEW MEXICO:	RESIDENCE.	SALARY.
Chief Justice.		
Samuel B. Axtell	Santa Fe	$3,000
Associate Justices.		
1. Joseph Bell	Albuquerque	3,000
2. Warren Bristol	Deming	3,000

UTAH:—		
Chief Justice.		
John A. Hunter	Salt Lake City	3,000
Associate Justices.		
1. Philip H. Emerson	Ogden	3,000
2. Stephen P. Twiss	Beaver City	3,000

WASHINGTON:—		
Chief Justice.		
Roger S. Green	Olympia	3,000
Associate Justices.		
1. John P. Hoyt	Olympia	3,000
2. Sam'l S. Wingard	Walla Walla	3,000

WYOMING:—		
Chief Justice.		
James B. Sener	Cheyenne	3,000
Associate Justices.		
1. Jacob B. Blair	Laramie City	3,000
2. Samuel C. Parks	Cheyenne	3,000

FORTY-EIGHTH CONGRESS.

Expires March 4th, 1885.

SENATE.

	Term Expires.
ALABAMA.	
John Pugh, D.	1885
John T. Morgan, D.	1889
ARKANSAS.	
A. H. Garland, D.	1889
J. D. Walker, D.	1885
CALIFORNIA.	
J. T. Farley, D.	1885
John F. Miller, R.	1887
COLORADO.	
Thomas J. Bowen, R.	1889
Nathaniel P. Hill, R.	1885
CONNECTICUT.	
Orville H. Platt, R.	1885
Joseph R. Hawley, R.	1887
DELAWARE.	
Thomas F. Bayard, D.	1887
Eli Saulsbury, D.	1889
FLORIDA.	
Charles W. Jones, D.	1887
Wilkinson Call, D.	1885
GEORGIA	
Alfred H. Colquitt, D.	1889
Joseph E. Brown, D.	1885
ILLINOIS.	
S. M. Cullom, R.	1889
John A. Logan, R.	1885
INDIANA.	
Daniel W. Voorhees, D.	1885
Ben. Harrison, R.	1887
IOWA.	
James F. Wilson, R.	1889
Wm. B. Allison, R.	1885
KANSAS.	
Preston B. Plumb, R.	1889
John J. Ingalls, R.	1885
KENTUCKY.	
James S. Beck, D.	1889
John S. Williams, D.	1885

	Term Expires.
LOUISIANA.	
B. J. Jonas, D.	1885
Randall Gibson, D.	1889
MAINE.	
Eugene Hale, R.	1887
Wm. P. Frye, R.	1889
MARYLAND.	
James B. Groeme, D.	1885
Arthur P. Gorman, D.	1887
MASSACHUSETTS.	
Henry L. Dawes, R.	1887
George F. Hoar, R.	1889
MICHIGAN.	
Thomas W. Palmer, R.	1889
Omar G. Conger, R.	1887
MINNESOTA.	
J. R. McMillan, R.	1887
Dwight M. Sabin, R.	1889
MISSISSIPPI.	
James Z. George, D.	1887
L. Q. C. Lamar, D.	1889
MISSOURI.	
Francis M. Cockrell, D.	1887
George C. Vest, D.	1885
NEBRASKA.	
C. F. Manderson, R.	1889
Charles H. Van Wyck, R.	1887
NEVADA.	
John P. Jones, R.	1885
James G. Fair, D.	1887
NEW HAMPSHIRE.	
Austin F. Pike, R.	1889
Henry W. Blair, R.	1885
NEW JERSEY.	
J. R. McPherson, D.	1889
Wm. J. Sewell, R.	1887
NEW YORK.	
Warner Miller, R.	1878
Eldridge Lapham, R.	1885

NORTH CAROLINA.

	Term Expires.
Matt Ransom, D.	1889
Zebulon B. Vance, D.	1885

OHIO.

George H. Pendleton, D.	1885
John Sherman, R.	1887

OREGON.

J. N. Dolph, R.	1889
James H. Slater, D.	1885

PENNSYLVANIA.

J. Donald Cameron, R.	1885
John I. Mitchell, R.	1887

RHODE ISLAND.

Nelson B. Aldrich, R.	1887
Henry B. Anthony, R.	1889

SOUTH CAROLINA.

Matthew C. Butler, D.	1889
Wade Hampton, D.	1885

TENNESSEE.

	Term Expires.
Isham G. Harris, D.	1889
H. E. Jackson, D.	1887

TEXAS.

Richard Coke, D.	1889
Samuel B. Maxey, D.	1887

VERMONT.

Justin S. Morrill, R.	1885
George F. Edmunds, R.	1887

VIRGINIA.

William Mahone, Readj	1887
H. H. Riddleberger, Readj.	1889

WEST VIRGINIA.

John E. Kenna, D.	1889
J. N. Camden, D.	1887

WISCONSIN.

Angus Cameron, R.	1885
Philetus Sawyer, R.	1887

RECAPITULATION.

Democrats	36
Republicans	38
Readjusters	2
Total	76

FORTY-EIGHTH CONGRESS.

Expires March 4th, 1885.

HOUSE OF REPRESENTATIVES.

ALABAMA.

1 James T. Johns. D.
2 H. A. Herbert. D.
3 W. C. Oates. D.
4 Charles M. Shelley. D.
5 T. Williams. D.
6 G. W. Hewett. D.
7 W. H. Forney. D.
8 Luke Pryor. D.

ARKANSAS.

Congressman-at-Large:

C. R. Breckinridge. D.

1 P. Dunn. D.
2 James K. Jones. D.
3 John H. Rogers. D.
4 Samuel W. Pell. D.

CALIFORNIA.

Congressmen-at-Large:

CHAS. A. SUMNER. D.
JOHN R. GLASCOCK. D.
1 W. S. Rosecrans. D.
2 J. H. Budd. D.
3 Barclay Henry. D.
4 P. B. Tulley. D.

COLORADO.

1 James B. Belford. R.

CONNECTICUT.

1 W. W. Eaton. D.
2 Chas. L. Mitchell. D.
3 John T. Wait. R.
4 Ed. W. Seymour. D.

DELAWARE.

1 Chas. B. Love. D.

FLORIDA.

1 R. H. M. Davidson. D.
2 Horatio Bisbee, Jr. R.

GEORGIA.

Congressmen-at-Large:

THOS. HARDEMAN. D.
1 John C. Nicholls. D.
2 H. G. Turner. D.
3 Chas. F. Crisp. D.
4 H. M. Buchanan. D.
5 N. J. Hammond. D.
5 J. H. Blount. D.
7 Judson C. Clements. D.
8 Seaborn Reese. D.
9 Allen D. Candles. D.

ILLINOIS.

1 Ransom W. Denman. R.
2 John J. Finerty. D.
3. Geo. R. Davis. R.
4 Geo. E. Adams. R.
5 Reuben Ellwood. R.
6 R. R. Hitt. R.
7 T. J. Henderson. R.
8 Wm. Cullen. R.
9 L. E. Payson. R.
10 N. E. Worthington. D.
11 W. H. Neece. D.
12 Jas. W. Riggs. D.
13 Wm. M. Springer. D.
14 J. H. Rowell. R.
15. J. G. Cannon. R.
16 Aaron Shaw. D.
17 Samuel W. Moulton. D.
18 W. R. Morrison. D.
19 R. W. Townsend. D.
20 J. R. Thomas. R.

INDIANA.

1 J. J. Kleiner. D.
2 Thomas R. Cobb. D.
3 S. M. Stockslager. D.
4 W. S. Holman. D.
5 C. C. Matson. D.
6 T. M. Browne. R.
7 S. J. Peele. R.
8 John E. Lamb. D.
9 Thos. B. Ward. D.
10 Thos. J. Wood. D.
11 George W. Steele. R.
12 Robert Lowry. D.
13 W. H. Calkins. R.

IOWA.

1 M. A. McCoid. R.
2 Jeremiah H. Murphy. D.
3 David B. Henderson. R.
4 L. H. Weller. D.
5 Benj. T. Frederick. D.
6 J. C. Cook. D.
7 John Kasson. R.
8 W. P. Hepburn. R.
9 W. H. M. Pusey. D.
10 Adoniram J. Holmes. R.
11 Isaac S. Struble. R.

KANSAS.

Congressmen-at-Large:

E. N. MORRILL. R.
LEWIS HANBACK. R.
SAMUEL R. PETERS. R.
BISHOP W. PERKINS. R.
1 John A. Anderson. R.
2 Dudley C. Haskell. R.
3 Thomas Ryan. R.

KENTUCKY.

1 Oscar Turner. I. D.
2 James F. Clay. D.
3 John E. Halsell. D.
4 Thos. H. Robertson. D.
5 Albert S. Willis. D.
6 J. G. Carlisle. D.
7 J. C. S. Blackburn. D.
8 P. B. Thompson, Jr. D.
9 W. W. Culbertson. R.
10. John D. White. R.
11 Frank Wolford. D.

LOUISIANA.

1 Carleton Hunt. D.
2 John Ellis. D.
3 Taylor Beattie. D.
4 N. C. Blanchard. D.
5 J. F. King. D.
6 Ed. T. Lewis. D.

MAINE.

Congressmen-at-Large.

Thos. B. Reed. R.
Nelson Dingley. R.
Chas. A. Boutelle. R.
Seth D. Milliken. R.

MARYLAND

1 G. W. Covington. D
2 J. F. C. Talbot. D.
3 F. S. Hoblitzell. D.
4 J. V. L. Findlay. D.
5 Hart. B. Holton. R.
6 Louis E. McComas. R.

MASSACHUSETTS.

1 Robert T. Davis. R.
2 John D. Long. R.
3 A. A. Ranney. R.
4 P. A. Collins. D.
5 Leopold Morse. D.
6 Henry B. Levering. D.
7 Eben F. Stone. R.
8 Wm. A. Russell. R.
9 Theodore Lyman. Ind.
10 Wm. W. Rice. R.
11 Wm. Whiting. R.
12 Vacant.

MICHIGAN.

1 Wm. C. Maybury. D.
2 N. B. Eldridge. D.
3 Edward S. Lacey. R.
4 Geo. L. Yaple. D.
5 Julius Houseman. D.
6 Edwin B. Winans. D.
7 Ezra C. Carleton. D.
8 Roswell G. Herr. R.
9 Byron M. Cutcheon. R.
10 H. H. Hatch. R.
11 Edward Breitung. R.

MINNESOTA.

1 Melville White. R.
2 James B. Wakefield. R.
3 H. B. Strait. R.
4 W. D. Washburn. R.
5 Knute Nelson. R.

MISSISSIPPI.

1 H. L. Muldrow. D.
2 Van H. Manning. D. (Contested).
3 E. S. Jeffords. R.
4 H. D. Money. D.
5 O. R. Singleton. D.
6 H. S. Van Eaton. D.
7 E. Barksdale. D.

MISSOURI.

1 W. W. Hatch. D.
2 H. M. Alexander. D.
3 A. M. Dockery. D.
4 James N. Burnes. D.
5 Alex. Graves. D.
6 J. Cosgrove. D.
7 A. H. Buckner. D.
8 J. J. O'Neil. D.
9 J. H. McLean. R.
10 M. L. Clardy. D.
11 R. P. Bland. D.
12 C. H. Morgan. D.
13 R. W. Ryan. D.
14 L. H. Davis. D.

NEBRASKA.

1 A. J. Weaver. R.
2 James Laird. R.
3 E. R. Valentine. R.

NEVADA.

George W. Cassidy. D.

NEW HAMPSHIRE.

1 Martin A. Haynes. R.
2 Ossian Ray. R.

NEW JERSEY.

1 Thomas M. Ferrell. D.
2 J. H. Brewer. R.
3 John Kean, Jr. R.
4 Benjamin F. Howey. R.
5 William Walter Phelps. R.
6 W. H. F. Fiedler. D.
7 William McAdoo. D.

NEW YORK.

Congressmen-at-Large.

Henry W. Slocum. D.
1 Perry Belmont. D.
2 William E. Robinson. D.
3 Darwin R. James. R.
4 Felix Campbell. D.
5 Nicholas Muller. D.
6 Samuel S. Cox. D.
7 William Dorsheimer. D.

8 John J. Adams. D.
9 John Hardy. D.
10 A. S. Hewitt. D.
11 Orlando B. Potter. D.
12 Waldo Hutchins. D.
13 J. H. Ketcham. R.
14 Lewis Beach. D.
15 John H. Bagley, Jr. D.
16 T. J. Van Alstyne. D.
17 Henry G. Burleigh. R.
18 Frederick A. Johnson. R.
19 A. X. Parker. R.
20 Ed. Wemple. D.
21 George W. Ray. R.
22 Charles H. Skinner. R.
23 J. Thomas Spriggs. D.
24 Newton W. Nutting. R.
25 Frank Hiscock. R.
26 Sereno E. Payne. R.
27 James W. Wadsworth. R.
28 Stephen C. Millard. R.
29 John Arnot. D.
30 H. S. Greenleaf. D.
31 Robert S. Stevens. D.
32 William F. Rodgers. D.
33 Francis B. Brewer. R.

NORTH CAROLINA.

Congressman-at-Large:

R. S. BENNETT. D.
1 Vacant.
2 J. E. O'Hara. R.
3 W. J. Green. D.
4 W. R. Cox. D.
5 Alfred M. Scales. D.
6 Clement Dowd. D.
7 Tyre York. R.
8 R. B. Vance. D.

OHIO.

1 John F. Follett. D.
2 Isaac M. Jordan. D.
3 H. L. Morey. R.
4 Benjamin La Fevre. D.
5 George E. Seney. D.
6 William D. Hill. D.
7 John P. Leedom. D.
8 J. Werren Keifer. R.
9 J. S. Robinson. R.
10 Frank H. Hurd. D.
11 J. W. McCormick. R.
12 Alphonso Hart. R.
13 George R. Converse. D.
14 G. W. Geddes. D.
15 A. J. Werner. R.
16 Beriah Wilkins. D
17 J. D. Taylor. R.
18 William McKinley, Jr. R.
19 Ezra B. Taylor. R.
20 David R. Paige. D.
21 Martin A. Foran. D.

OREGON.

M. C. George. R.

PENNSYLVANIA.

Congressman-at-Large.

MORTIMER F. ELLIOTT. D.
1 H. H. Bingham. R.
2 Charles O'Neill. R.
3 Samuel J. Randall. D.
4 William D. Kelley. R.
5 A. C. Harmer. R.
6 James B. Everhardt. R.
7 Isaac N. Evans. R.
8 D. Ermentrout. D.
9 A. Herr Smith. R.
10 William Mutchler. D.
11 John B. Storm. D.
12 D. W. Connolly. D.
13 C. N. Brumm. R. G.
14 Samuel F. Barr. R.
15 George A. Post. D.
16 W. W. Brown. R.
17 J. M. Campbell. R.
18 L. E. Atkinson. R.
19 William A. Duncan. D.
20 A. D. Curtin. D.
21 C. E. Boyle. D.
22 James A. Hopkins. D.
23 Thomas M. Bayne. R.
24 George V. Lawrence. R.
25 J. D. Patton. D.
26 S. H. Miller. R.
27 S. M. Brainerd. R.

RHODE ISLAND.

1 Henry J. Spooner. R.
2 Jonathan Chase. R.

SOUTH CAROLINA.

1 Samuel Dibble. D.
2 George D. Tillman. D.
3 D. W. Aiken. D.
4 John H. Evans. D.
5 John J. Hemphill. D.
6 George W. Dargon. D.
7 E. W. M. Mackey. R.

TENNESSEE.

1 A. H. Pettibone. R.
2 L. C. Houck. R.
3 George C. Dibrell. D.
4 B. McMillen. D.
5 James D. Tillman. D.
6 A. J. Caldwell. D.
7 John G. Ballentine. D.
8 John M. Taylor. D.
9 Rice A. Pierce. D.
10 Casey Young. D.

TEXAS.

1 Charles Stewart. D.
2 J. H. Regan. D.
3 James H. Jones. D.
4 David B. Culberson. D.
5 John W. Throckmorton. D.
6 Olin Wellborn. D.
7 Thomas P. Ochiltree. R.
8 J. F. Miller. D.
9 John M. Taylor. D.
10 John Hancock. D.
11 W T. D. Lanham. D.

VERMONT.

1 John W. Stuart. R.
2 Luke P. Poland. R.

VIRGINIA.

Congressman-at-Large.

John S. Wise, Readj.
1 R W. Mayo. Readj.
2 H. H. Libby. Readj.
3 George D. Wise. D.
4 B. S. Hooper. Readj.
5 George C. Cabell. D.
6 J. R. Tucker. D.
7 Vacant.
8 J. S Barbour. D.
9 Henry Bowen. Readj.

WEST VIRGINIA.

1 Nathan Goff. R.
2 William L. Winans. D.
3 C. P. Snyder. D.
4 Eustace Gibson. D.

WISCONSIN.

1 John Wilson. D.
2 D. H. Sumner. D.
3 Burr W. Jones. D.
4 P. V. Deuster. D
5 Joseph Rankin. D.
6 R. Guenther. R.
7 G. M. Woodward. D.
8 William T. Price. R.
9 Isaac Stephenson. R.

RECAPITULATION.

Regular Democrats	195
Republicans	119
Readjusters	4
Greenbackers	1
Independent	1
Independent Republican	1
Independent Democrat	1
Vacant	3
Total	325

TERRITORIAL DELEGATES.

ARIZONA.

G. H Ouray. D.

DAKOTA.

John B. Raymond. R.

IDAHO.

T. F. Singsler. R.

MONTANA.

Martin Maginnis.

NEW MEXICO

T. Luna. R.

UTAH.

John T. Cain. D.

WASHINGTON.

Thomas H. Brents. R

WYOMING

M. E. Post. D.

VOTE FOR PRESIDENT FROM 1864 TO 1880.

STATES.	1864.		1868.		1872.		1876		1880.	
	Lincoln.	McClellan	Grant.	Seymour.	Grant.	Greeley.	Hayes.	Tilden.	Garfield.	Hancock.
	Rep.	Dem.	Rep.	Dem.	Rep.	Lib.	Rep.	Dem.	Rep.	Dem.
Alabama	......	......	76,366	77,088	90,272	79,444	68,230	102,002	56,221	91,185
Arkansas	......	......	22,112	19,078	41,373	37,927	38,669	58,071	42,436	60,775
California	62,134	44,841	54,583	54,077	54,020	40,718	78,614	75,845	80,378	80,417
Colorado	......	......	......	......	......	......	By Legislature.		27,450	26,647
Connecticut	44,691	42,285	50,995	47,952	50,638	45,880	59,034	61,934	67,071	64,415
Delaware	8,155	8,767	7,623	10,980	11,115	10,206	10,752	13,381	14,133	15,275
Florida	......	......	Legislature.		17,763	15,427	23,849	22,923	23,632	27,022
Georgia	......	......	57,134	102,722	62,550	76,356	50,446	130,088	51,086	102,470
Illinois	189,496	158,730	250,303	199,143	241,944	184,938	278,232	258,601	318,037	277,321
Indiana	150,422	130,233	176,548	166,980	186,147	163,632	208,011	213,526	232,164	225,522
Iowa	89,075	49,596	120,399	74,040	131,366	71,196	171,327	112,099	183,927	105,845
Kansas	16,441	3,691	31,048	13,990	67,048	32,970	78,322	37,902	121,549	59,801
Kentucky	27,786	64,301	39,566	115,890	88,766	99,995	97,156	159,690	106,306	149,068
Louisiana	......	......	33,263	80,225	71,663	57,029	75,135	70,636	38,016	65,067
Maine	61,803	44,211	70,493	42,460	61,422	29,087	66,300	49,823	74,039	65,171
Maryland	40,153	32,739	30,438	62,357	66,760	67,687	71,981	91,780	78,515	93,706
Massachusetts	126,742	48,745	136,477	59,408	133,472	59,260	150,063	108,777	165,205	111,960
Michigan	91,521	74,604	128,550	97,069	138,455	78,355	166,534	141,095	185,341	131,597
Minnesota	25,060	17,375	43,545	28,075	55,117	34,423	72,992	48,799	93,903	53,315
Mississippi	......	......	......	......	82,175	47,288	52,605	112,173	34,854	75,750
Missouri	72,750	31,678	86,860	65,628	119,196	151,434	145,029	203,077	153,567	208,609
Nebraska	......	......	9,729	5,439	18,329	7,812	31,916	17,554	54,979	28,523
Nevada	9,826	6,594	6,480	5,218	8,413	6,236	10,383	9,308	10,445	11,215
New Hampshire	36,400	32,871	38,191	31,224	37,168	31,424	41,539	38,509	44,852	40,794
New Jersey	60,723	68,024	80,121	83,001	91,656	76,456	103,517	115,962	120,555	122,565
New York	368,735	361,986	419,883	429,883	440,736	387,281	489,207	521,949	555,544	534,511
North Carolina	......	......	96,769	84,601	94,769	70,094	108,417	125,427	115,874	124,208
Ohio	265,154	205,568	280,223	238,606	281,852	244,321	330,698	323,182	375,048	340,821
Oregon	9,888	8,457	10,961	11,125	11,819	7,730	15,206	11,149	20,619	19,855

VOTE FOR PRESIDENT FROM 1864 TO 1880—(*Continued*).

STATES.	1864. Lincoln. *Rep.*	1864. McClellan *Dem.*	1868. Grant. *Rep.*	1868. Seymour. *Dem.*	1872. Grant. *Rep.*	1872. Greeley. *Lib.*	1876. Hayes. *Rep.*	1876. Tilden. *Dem.*	1880. Garfield. *Rep.*	1880. Hancock. *Dem.*
Pennsylvania	296,391	276,316	342,280	313,382	349,589	212,041	384,122	366,148	444,704	407,428
Rhode Island	13,692	8,470	12,993	6,548	13,665	5,329	15,787	10,712	18,195	10,779
South Carolina	......	......	62,301	45,237	72,290	22,703	91,870	90,906	58,071	112,312
Tennessee	......	......	56,628	26,129	85,655	94,391	89,566	133,166	107,677	129,569
Texas	......	......	......	......	47,406	66,500	44,800	104,755	57,893	156,428
Vermont	42,419	13,321	44,167	12,045	41,481	10,927	44,092	20,254	45,567	18,316
Virginia	......	......	......	......	93,468	91,654	95,558	139,670	84,020	128,586
West Virginia	23,152	10,438	29,175	20,306	32,315	29,451	42,698	56,455	46,243	57,391
Wisconsin	83,458	65,884	108,857	84,707	104,997	86,477	130,668	123,927	144,400	114,649
Total	2,216,067	1,808,725	3,015,071	3,709,613	3,597,070	2,834,079	4,033,295	4,284,265	4,450,921	4,447,888
Majority	407,342		305,458		762,991		Over all.	157,394	3,033	

Total vote in 1824	352,062	Total vote in 1856	4,053,967
" 1828	1,156,328	" 1860	4,676,853
" 1832	1,217,691	" 1864	4,024,792
" 1836	1,498,205	" 1868	5,724,686
" 1840	2,410,772	" 1872	6,431,149
" 1844	2,698,458	" 1876	8,411,139
" 1848	2,872,896	" 1880	9,242,595
" 1852	3,142,877		

ELECTIONS.

VOTE FOR PRESIDENT FROM 1852 TO 1860.

STATES.	1852. Scott. *Whig.*	1852. Pierce. *Dem.*	1852. Hale. *Free Soil.*	1856. Fremont *Rep.*	1856. Buch'n. *Dem*	1856. Fillmore *Amer'n.*	1860. Lincoln. *Rep.*	1860. Douglas. *Dem.*	1860. Breck. *Dem.*	1860. Bell. *Union.*
Alabama	15,038	26,881			46,739	28,552		13,651	48,831	27,825
Arkansas	7,404	12,173			21,910	10,787		5,227	28,732	20,094
California	35,407	40,626	100	20,691	53,365	36,165	39,173	38,516	34,334	6,817
Connecticut	30,357	33,249	3,160	42,715	34,995	2,615	43,692	15,522	14,641	3,291
Delaware	6,293	6,318	62	308	8,004	6,175	3,815	1,023	7,317	3,864
Florida	2,875	4,318			6,358	4,833		367	8,543	5,437
Georgia	16,660	34,705			56,578	42,228		11,590	51,889	42,886
Illinois	64,934	80,597	9,966	96,180	105,348	37,444	172,161	160,215	2,404	3,913
Indiana	80,901	95,340	6,929	94,375	118,670	22,386	139,033	115,509	12,295	5,305
Iowa	15,856	17,763	1,604	43,954	36,170	9,180	70,409	55,111	1,043	1,763
Kentucky	57,068	53,806		314	74,642	67,416	1,364	25,651	53,143	66,058
Louisiana	17,255	18,647			22,161	20,709		7,625	22,681	20,204
Maine	32,543	41,609	8,030	67,379	39,080	3,325	62,811	26,693	6,368	2,046
Maryland	35,066	40,020	54	281	39,115	47,460	2,294	5,966	42,482	41,766
Massachusetts	52,683	44,569	28,023	108,190	39,240	19,626	106,533	34,372	5,998	22,331
Michigan	33,859	41,842	7,237	71,772	52,136	1,660	88,480	65,057	805	405
Minnesota							22,069	11,920	748	62
Mississippi	17,548	26,776			35,446	24,195		3,283	40,797	25,040
Missouri	29,984	38,353			58,164	48,524	17,028	58,801	31,317	58,372
New Hampshire	16,147	29,997	6,695	38,345	32,789	422	37,519	25,881	2,112	441
New Jersey	38,556	44,305	350	28,338	46,943	24,115	58,324	62,801		
New York	234,882	262,083	25,329	276,007	195,878	124,604	362,646	312,510		
North Carolina	39,058	39,744			48,246	36,886		2,701	48,332	44,990
Ohio	152,526	169,220	31,682	187,497	170,874	28,126	231,610	187,232	11,405	12,194
Oregon							5,270	3,951	3,006	183
Pennsylvania	179,174	198,568	8,525	147,510	230,710	82,175	268,030	16,765	178,871	12,776
Rhode Island	7,626	8,735	644	11,467	6,680	1,675	12,244	7,707		
Tennessee	58,898	57,018			73,638	66,178		11,350	64,709	69,274
Texas	4,945	13,552			31,169	15,639			47,548	15,438
Vermont	22,173	13,044	8,621	39,561	10,569	545	33,808	6,849	218	1,969
Virginia	58,572	73,858		291	89,706	60,310	1,929	16,290	74,323	74,681
Wisconsin	22,240	33,658	8,814	66,090	52,843	579	86,110	65,021	888	161
Total	1,386,578	1,601,474	155,825	1,341,264	1,838,169	874,534	1,866,352	1,375,157	845,763	589,581

MISCELLANEOUS.

NAMES OF THE SPEAKERS OF THE HOUSE OF REPRESENTATIVES— 1789 TO 1881.

1st Congress. — FREDERICK AUGUSTUS MUHLENBURGH, of Pennsylvania, was elected Speaker of the House of Representatives April 1, 1789, and served to March 3, 1791.

2d Congress. —JONATHAN TRUMBULL, of Connecticut, was elected Speaker, and served from the 24th of October, 1791, to March 3, 1793.

3d Congress. — FREDERICK AUGUSTUS MUHLENBURGH, of Pennsylvania, was elected Speaker, and served from December 2, 1793, to 3d of March, 1795.

4th and 5th Congresses.—JONATHAN DAYTON, of New Jersey, was elected Speaker, and served from the 7th of December, 1795, to 3d of March, 1799.

6th Congress,—THEODORE SEDGWICK, of Massachusetts, was elected Speaker, and served from the 2d of December, 1799, to 3d of March, 1801.

7th, 8th and 9th Congresses. —NATHANIEL MACON, of North Carolina, was elected Speaker, and served from 7th of December, 1801, to March 3, 1807.

10th and 11th Congresses,—JOSEPH B. VARNUM, of Massachusetts, was elected Speaker, and served from October 26, 1807, to 3d of March, 1811.

12th, 13th, 14th, 15th and 16th Congresses.— Henry Clay was elected Speaker, and served from 4th of November, 1811, to 3d of March, 1821.

17th Congress.—PHILIP P. BARBOUR, of Virginia, was elected Speaker, and served from 3d of December, 1821, to 3d of March, 1823.

18th Congress. —HENRY CLAY, of Kentucky, was elected Speaker, and served from 1st of December, 1823, to March 3, 1825.

19th Congress.—JOHN W. TAYLOR, of New York, was elected Speaker, and served from December 5, 1825, to March 2, 1827.

20th, 21st, 22d and 23d Congresses. — ANDREW STEPHENSON, of Virginia, was elected Speaker, and served from 3d of December, 1827, to 3d of June, 1834; and JOHN BELL, of Tennessee, was on the 4th of June, 1834, elected to serve out the balance of the 23d Congress, which ended on the 3d of March, 1835.

24th and 25th Congresses. —JAMES K. POLK, of Tennessee, was elected Speaker, and served from the 7th of December, 1835, to March 3, 1839.

26th Congress.—ROBERT M. T. HUNTER, of Virginia, was elected Speaker, and served from 16th December, 1839, to March 3, 1841.

27th Congress.—JOHN WHITE, of Kentucky, was elected Speaker, and served from 31st of May, 1841, to March 3, 1843.

28th Congress. —JOHN W. JONES, of Virginia, was elected Speaker, and served from 4th of December, 1843, to March 3, 1845.

29th Congress.—JOHN W. DAVIS, of Indiana, was elected Speaker, and served from 1st of December, 1845, to March 3, 1847.

30th Congress. — ROBERT C. WINTHROP, of Massachusetts, was elected Speaker, and served from 6th of December, 1847, to March 3, 1849.

31st Congress. —HOWELL COBB, of Georgia, was elected Speaker, and served from 24th of December, 1849, to March 3, 1851.

32d and 33d Congresses.—LINN BOYD, of Kentucky, was elected Speaker, and served from 4th of December, 1851, to March 3, 1855.

34th Congress. —NATHANIEL P. BANKS, Jr., of Massachusetts, was elected Speaker, and served from February 2, 1857, to March 3, 1857.

35th Congress. —JAMES L. ORR, of South Carolina, was elected Speaker, and served from December 7, 1856, to March 3, 1859.

36th Congress.—WILLIAM PENDLETON, of New Jersey, was elected Speaker, February 1, 1860, and served to March 3, 1861.

37th Congress.—GALUSHA A. GROW, of Pennsylvania, was elected Speaker, July 4, 1861, and served to March 3, 1863.

38th, 39th and 40th Congresses.—SCHUYLER COLFAX, of Indiana, was elected Speaker, December 7, 1863, and served to March 3, 1869.

41st Congress.—JAMES G. BLAINE, of Maine, was elected Speaker, March 4, 1869, and served to March 4, 1871.

42d Congress.—JAMES G. BLAINE, of Maine, was elected Speaker, March 4, 1871, and served to March 3, 1873.

43d Congress.—JAMES G. BLAINE, of Maine, was elected Speaker, December 1, 1873, and served to March 3, 1875.

44th Congress.—MICHAEL C. KERR, of Indiana, was elected Speaker, December 6, 1875. Died August 19, 1876.

44th Congress. SAMUEL J. RANDALL, of Pennsylvania, was elected Speaker, December 4, 1876, in place of Kerr, deceased.

45th Congress.—SAMUEL J. RANDALL, of Pennsylvania, was elected Speaker, October 15, 1877.

46th Congress.—SAMUEL J. RANDALL, of Pennsylvania, was elected Speaker, March 18, 1879.

47th Congress.—JOSEPH W. KEIFER, of Ohio, was elected Speaker, December 5, 1881.

48th Congress.—JOHN G. CARLISLE, of Kentucky, was elected Speaker, December 3, 1883.

PRESIDENTS AND VICE-PRESIDENTS OF THE UNITED STATES.

PRESIDENTS.

YEAR OF QUALIFICATION.	NAME.	WHERE FROM.	TERM OF OFFICE.
1789..........	George Washington........	Virginia............	8 years.
1797..........	John Adams..............	Massachusetts......	4 years.
1801..........	Thomas Jefferson.........	Virginia............	8 years.
1809..........	James Madison..........	Virginia............	8 veers.
1817..........	James Monroe...........	Virginia............	8 years.
1824..........	John Quincy Adams.......	Massachusetts......	4 years.
1829..........	Andrew Jackson..........	Tennessee..........	8 years.
1837..........	Martin Van Buren........	New York..........	4 years.
1841..........	William Henry Harrison*..	Ohio.............	1 month.
1841..........	John Tyler.............	Virginia............	3 years, 11 mos.
1845..........	James Knox Polk.........	Tennessee..........	4 years.
1849..........	Zachary Taylor†	Louisiana..........	4 months, 5 days.
1850..........	Millard Fillmore.........	New York..........	3 yrs. 7 ms. 26 dys.
1853..........	Franklin Pierce..........	New Hampshire....	4 years.
1857..........	James Buchanan.........	Pennsylvania.......	4 years.
1861..........	Abraham Lincoln‡........	Illinois...........	4 yrs., 1 m., 10 dys.
1865..........	Andrew Johnson.........	Tennessee.........	3 yrs. 10 m. 20 dys.
1869..........	Ulysses S. Grant.........	Illinois...........	8 years.
1877..........	Rutherford B. Hayes......	Ohio.............	4 years.
1881..........	James A. Garfield•.......	Ohio.............	6 months, 15 days.
1881..........	Chester A. Arthur........	New York..........	3 yrs., 5 m. 15 dys.

*Died in office, April 4, 1841, when Vice-President Tyler succeeded him.
†Died in office, April 9, 1850, when Vice-President Fillmore succeeded him.
‡Assassinated, April 14, 1865, when Vice-President Johnson succeeded him.
• Assassinated, July 2, 1881. Died Sept. 19, 1881, when Vice-President Arthur succeeded him.

VICE-PRESIDENTS.

YEAR OF QUALIFICATION.	NAME.	WHERE FROM.
1789	John Adams	Massachusetts.
1797	Thomas Jefferson	Virginia.
1801	Aaron Burr	New York.
1804	George Clinton	New York.
1813	Eldridge Gerry	Massachusetts.
1817	Daniel D. Tompkins	New York.
1824	John C. Calhoun	South Carolina.
1833	Martin Van Buren	New York.
1837	Richard M. Johnson	Kentucky.
1841	John Tyler	Virginia.
1842	Samuel L. Southard§	New Jersey.
1845	George M. Dallas	Pennsylvania.
1849	Millard Fillmore	New York.
1851	William R. King§	Alabama.
1853	David R. Atchison	Missouri.
1855	Jesse D. Bright§	Indiana.
1857	John C. Breckinridge	Kentucky.
1861	Hannibal Hamlin	Maine.
1865	Andrew Johnson	Tennessee.
1865	Lafayette S. Foster.§	Connecticut.
1869	Schuyler Colfax	Indiana.
1873	Henry Wilson‖	Massachusetts.
1875	Thomas W. Ferry§	Michigan.
1877	William A. Wheeler	New York.
1881	Chester A. Arthur*	New York.
1881	David Davis*	Illinois.
1883	George F. Edmunds	Vermont.

*Died in office, Nov. 22, 1875.
§*Ex-officio* as President *pro tem*, of Senate.
¶Succeeded James A. Garfield, assassinated July 2, 1881.]

LEGAL HOLIDAYS IN VARIOUS STATES.

July 4 [INDEPENDENCE DAY,] and December 25 [CHRISTMAS DAY], together with THANKSGIVING DAY, [usually last Thursday in November], and Fast Days, whenever appointed, are legal holidays in all States.

January 1 [NEW YEAR'S DAY], in all States except Arkansas, Delaware, Georgia, Kentucky, Maine, Massachusetts, New Hampshire, North Carolina, Rhode Island and South Carolina.

February 22 [WASHINGTON'S BIRTHDAY], in all States except Alabama, Arkansas, Florida, Illinois, Indiana, Iowa, Kansas, Maine, Missouri, North Carolina, Ohio, Oregon, Tennessee and Texas.

General Election Day (generally on Tuesday after first Monday in November), in California, Maine, Missouri, New Jersey, New York, Oregon, South Carolina and Wisconsin.

Decoration Day (May 30), is in Colorado, Connecticut, Maine, Michigan, New Hampshire, New Jersey, New York, Pennsylvania, Rhode Island and Vermont.

Good Friday (March 23) is in Florida, Louisiana, Minnesota and Pennsylvania.

Shrove Tuesday (February 6), Louisiana, cities of Mobile, Montgomery and Selma, Alabama.

Memorial Day (April 26) is in Georgia.

Anniversary of the Battle of New Orleans (January 8) is in Louisiana.

Lincoln's Birthday (February 12) is in Louisiana.

Firemen's Anniversary (March 4) is in Louisiana.

Anniversary of Texan Independence (March 2), and of Battle of San Jacinto (April 21) in Texas.

POPULATION AND DEBT OF CITIES OF UNITED STATES.

NAME OF PLACE.	Population Census 1880.	Debt 1880.	Debt for each person.
Akron, Ohio	16,511	$ 17,619	$ 1.06
Albany, N. Y.	90,903	3,138,500	34.52
Alleghany, Pa.	78 681	1,596,429	20.29
Allentown, Pa.	18,063	430,443	23.83
Alexandria, Va.	13,658	1,037,088	75.92
Altoona, Pa.	19,716	368,830	18.70
Amsterdam, N. Y.	11,711		
Atchison, Kan.	15,106	449,687	29.76
Atlanta, Ga.	34,398	2,180,000	63.38
Attleborough, Mass.	11,111	16,600	1.49
Auburn, N. Y.	22,924	530,000	23.12
Augusta Ga.	23,023	1,961,319	85.18
Aurora, Ill.	11,825	25,506	2.16
Austin, Texas	10,960	106,744	9.74
Baltimore, Md.	332,190	27,092,690	81.55
Bangor, Maine	16,827	2,661,000	158.13
Bay City, Mich.	20,693	433,100	20.93
Belleville, Ill.	10,682	217,712	20.38
Biddeford, Maine	12,652	183,874	14.53
Binghamton, N. Y.	17,315	299,500	17.29
Bloomington, Ill.	17,184	221,463	12.88
Boston, Mass.	362,535	28,244,017	77.90
Bridgeport, Conn.	29,145	831,000	28.51
Brockton, Mass.	13,608	71,200	5.23
Brooklyn, N. Y.	566,689	38,040,000	67.13
Buffalo, N. Y.	155,137	8,211,934	52.93
Burlington, Vt.	11,364	383,427	33.74
Burlington, Iowa	19,450	128,062	6.58
Cambridge, Mass.	52,740	3,403,723	64.53
Camden, N. J.	41,658	1,164,900	27.96
Canton, Ohio	12,258	180,657	14.73
Cedar Rapids, Iowa	10,104	40,876	4.04
Charleston, S. C.	49,999	4,129,102	82.58
Chattanooga, Tenn.	12,892	71,566	5.55
Chelsea, Mass.	21,785	1,554,496	71.35
Chester, Pa.	14,996	357,084	23.81
Chicago, Ill.	503,304	12,794,271	25.42
Cincinnati, Ohio	255,708	21,992,500	86.00
Cleveland, Ohio	160,142	4,076,946	25.45
Columbus, Ohio	51,665	1,259,162	24.37
Covington, Ky.	29,720	1,030,000	34.66
Cohoes, N. Y.	19,417	141,214	7.27
Council Bluffs, Iowa	18,059	138,400	7.66
Concord, N. H.	13,838	615,500	44.48
Chicopee, Mass.	11,325	100,050	8.83
Detroit, Mich.	116,342	1,282,772	11.02
Dayton, Ohio	38,677	1,101,520	28.48
Denver, Col.	35,630	20,000	56
Des Moines, Iowa	22,408	578,000	25.79
Dubuque, Iowa	22,254	804,611	36.15
Dover N. H.	11,687	458,830	39.25
Danbury, Conn.	11,669	255,415	21.88
Derby, Conn.	11,649	80,243	6.88
Dallos, Texas	10,358	304,356	29.36
Davenport, Iowa	21,834	290,675	13.12

POPULATION AND DEBT OF CITIES OF U. S.—CONTINUED.

NAME OF PLACE.	Population Census 1880.	Debt 1880.	Debt for each person.
Evansville, Ind.	29,280	None.	
Elizabeth, N. J.	28,229	$ 5,512,638	$195.28
Erie, Pa.	27,730	1,201,229	43.31
Elmira, N. Y.	20,541	270,100	13.17
East Saginaw, Mich.	19,016	611,055	32.13
Easton, Pa.	11,924	219,949	18.45
Eau Claire, Wis.	10,118	101,000	9.98
Fall River, Mass.	49,006	3,169,765	64.68
Fort Wayne, Ind.	26,880	856,990	31.87
Flushing, N. Y.	15,919		
Fond du Lac, Wis.	13,091	165,000	12.60
Fitchburg, Mass.	12,405	770,788	62.11
Fishkill, N. Y.	10,732		
Grand Rapids, Mich.	32,015	471,000	14.71
Galveston, Texas.	22,253	1,023,249	45.97
Gloucester, Mass.	19,329	193,370	10.00
Galesburg, Ill.	11,446	53,250	4.65
Hempstead, N. Y.	18,160		
Hartford, Conn.	42,553	3,689,855	86.71
Hoboken, N. J.	30,999	1,099,250	35.46
Harrisburg, Pa.	30,762	1,065,300	34.63
Holyoke, Mass.	21,851	878,454	40.20
Houston, Texas.	18,646	1,501,594	80.53
Haverhill, Mass.	18,475	393,428	21.29
Hamilton, Ohio.	12,122	48,067	3.96
Hannibal, Mo.	11,074	144,027	13.00
Indianapolis, Ind.	75,074	1,914,500	25.50
Jersey City, N. J.	120,728	15,598,435	129.16
Johnstown, N. Y.	16,626		
Joliet, Ill.	16,145	54,000	3.34
Jackson, Mich.	16,105	183,500	11.39
Jacksonville, Ill.	10,927	273,336	25.10
Jeffersonville, Ind.	10,422	240,350	23.06
Jamaica, N. Y.	10,089		
Kansas City, Mo.	55,813	1,339,224	23.99
Kingston, N. Y.	18,342	644,880	35.15
Keokuk, Iowa.	12,117	372,375	30.73
Kalamazoo, Mich.	11,937	25,000	2.09
Louisville, Ky.	123,645	4,842,365	39.16
Lowell, Mass.	59,485	1,554,275	26.12
Lawrence, Mass.	39,187	1,712,000	43.68
Lynn, Mass.	38,284	2,072,815	54.14
Lancaster, Pa.	25,769	464,142	18.04
Lewiston, Maine.	19,083	1,038,102	54.39
Long Island City, N. Y.	17,117	950,000	55.50
Lexington, Ky.	16,656	84,316	5.06
Leavenworth, Kan.	16,550	396,573	23.96
Lynchburg, Va.	15,959	794,847	49.80
Lafayette, Ind.	14,860	None.	
Leadville, Col.	14,820		
La Crosse, Wis.	14,505	135,000	9.30
Lincoln, R. I.	13,765	50,000	3.63
Lockport, N. Y.	13,522	108,667	8.03
Little Rock, Ark.	13,185	335,213	25.42
Lincoln, Neb.	13,004	199,615	15.35

POPULATION AND DEBT OF CITIES OF U. S.—CONTINUED.

NAME OF PLACE.	Population Census 1880.	Debt 1880.	Debt for each person.
Los Angeles, Cal.	11,311	$ 310,177	27.42
Logansport, Ind.	11,198	456,276	40.77
Lennox, N. Y	10,249		
Milwaukee, Wis.	115,578	2,160,289	18.69
Minneapolis, Minn.	46,887	1,137,467	24.25
Memphis, Tenn.	33,593	None.	
Manchester, N. H.	32,630	929,000	28.49
Mobile, Ala.	31,205	2,671,100	85.91
Meriden, Conn.	18,340	788,317	42.98
Montgomery, Ala.	16,714	567,900	33.91
Macon, Ga.	12,748	743,000	58.28
Malden, Mass.	12,017	483,523	40.23
Middletown, Conn.	11,731		
Muskegon, Mich.	11,262	180,000	15.98
Madison, Wis.	10,325	136,768	13.24
Marlborough, Mass.	10,126	151,951	15.00
Newburyport, Mass.	13,537	428,706	31.66
New York, N. Y.	1,206,590	109,425,414	90.69
New Orleans, La.	216,140		
Newark, N. J.	136,400	9,070,032	66.41
New Haven, Conn.	62,882	1,359,619	21.62
New Bedford, Mass.	26,875	1,086,000	40.37
Norfolk, Va.	21,966	2,187,371	99.57
Norwich, Conn.	21,141	1,191,256	56.34
Newport, Ky.	20,433	966,618	42.41
Newburgh, N. Y.	18,050	313,400	17.36
New Brunswick, N. J.	17,167	1,618,946	94.30
Newton, Mass.	16,995	993,591	58.46
New Albany, Ind.	16,422	358,482	21.82
Newport, R. I.	15,693	116,408	7.41
New Britain, Conn.	13,978	494,843	35.40
Norwalk, Conn.	13,956	522,495	37.43
New Lots, N. Y.	13,681		
Nashua, N. H.	13,397	458,661	34.23
Norristown, Pa.	13,064	81,200	6.21
Northampton, Mass.	12,172	537,500	44.15
New London, Conn.	10,529	496,611	47.16
North Adams, Mass.	10,192	267,894	26.28
Nashville, Tenn.	43,461	1,606,200	36.95
Oakland, Cal.	34,556	669,126	19.35
Omaha, Neb.	30,518	227,578	7.45
Oswego, N. Y.	21,117	1,264,224	59.86
Oshkosh, Wis.	15,749	130,500	8.28
Orange, N. J.	13,206	253,832	19.29
Oyster Bay, N. Y.	11,923		
Ogdensburg, N. Y.	10,340	135,000	13.05
Pittsburg, Pa.	156,381	14,134,296	90.37
Providence, R. I.	104,850		
Paterson, N. J.	50,887	1,359,500	26.71
Portland, Maine.	33,810	4,332,154	128.13
Peoria, Ill.	29,315	716,500	24.44
Petersburg, Va.	21,656	1,136,100	52.46
Poughkeepsie, N. Y.	20,207	1,939,198	95.96
Pawtucket, R. I.	19,030	935,000	49.13
Pittsfield, Mass.	13,367	385,341	28.82

POPULATION AND DEBT OF CITIES OF U. S.—CONTINUED.

NAME OF PLACE	Population Census 1880.	Debt 1880.	Debt for each person.
Portsmouth, Va	11,388	283,014	24.85
Portsmouth, Ohio	11,314	317,800	28.09
Philadelphia, Pa	846,984	16,251,636	19.18
Quincy, Ill	27,275	1,917,888	70.31
Quincy, Mass	10,529	65,980	62.66
Rochester, N. Y	89,363	5,701,686	63.80
Richmond, Va	63,803	4,399,021	68.95
Reading, Pa	43,280	999,000	23.08
Racine, Wis	16,031	218,512	13.63
Rockford, Ill	13,136	178,000	13.55
Richmond, Ind	12,743	167,000	13.10
Rutland, Vt	12,149	202,400	16.66
Rome, N. Y	12,045	160,000	13.28
Rock Island, Ill	11,660	289,650	24.78
St. Louis, Mo	350,222	22,847,761	65.18
San Francisco, Cal	232,956	3,059,285	13.12
Syracuse, N. Y	51,791	1,351,500	26.09
Scranton, Pa	45,850	325,202	7.09
St. Paul, Minn	41,498	1,526,715	36.74
Springfield, Mass	33,340	1,928,000	57.82
St. Joseph, Mo	32,484	2,445,600	73.71
Savannah, Ga	30,681	3,425,000	111.63
Salem, Mass	27,598	1,162,487	42.08
Somerville, Mass	24,985	1,586,978	63.56
Sacramento, Cal	21,420	861,000	40.19
Salt Lake City, Utah	20,768	67,000	3.22
Springfield, Ohio	20,729	58,627	2.82
San Antonio, Texas	20,561	155,266	7.55
Springfield, Ill	19,749	778,780	39.40
Sandusky, Ohio	15,838	381,215	24.07
Schnectady, N. Y	13,675	118,000	8.60
South Bend, Ind	13,279	337,000	25.30
San Jose, Cal	12,567	None.	
Steubenville, Ohio	12,093	30,190	2.91
Stamford, Conn	11,298	165,000	14.50
Shreveport, La	11,017		
Saratoga Springs, N. Y	10,822	297,600	27.50
Saugerties, N. Y	10,375		
Saginaw, Mich	10,525	202,800	19.00
Stockton, Cal	10,287	385,615	37.40
Shenandoah, Pa	10,148		
Troy, N. Y	56,747	958,296	16.80
Toledo, Ohio	50,143	3,232,060	64.46
Trenton, N. J	29,910	1,661,501	55.70
Terre Haute, Ind	26,040	267,224	10.26
Taunton, Mass	21,213	449,735	21.20
Topeka, Kan	15,451	333,249	21.50
Utica, N. Y	33,913	766,000	22.88
Virginia City, Nev	13,705	112,000	8.17
Vicksburg, Miss	11,814	373,218	31.59
Washington, D. C	147,307	23,310,146	158.25
Warwick, R. I	12,163	57,500	4.72
Worcester, Mass	58,295	2,447,543	41.98
Wilmington, Del	42,499	1,372,450	32.05
Wheeling, W. V	31,266	531,882	17.02

POPULATION AND DEBT OF CITIES OF U. S.—CONTINUED.

NAME OF PLACE.	Population Census 1880.	Debt 1880.	Debt for each person.
Wilkesbarre, Pa.	23,339	95,096	4.07
Watervliet (W. Troy), N. Y.	22,202		
Waterbury, Conn.	20,269	361,508	17.80
Williamsport, Pa.	18,934	651,272	34.40
Wilmington, N. C.	17,361	539,845	31.09
Woonsocket, R. I.	16,053	230,000	14.30
Wallkill, N. Y.	11,483		
Woburn, Mass.	10,938	626,602	57.26
Watertown, N. Y.	10,697	407,500	38.00
Weymouth, Mass.	10,571	64,392	6.09
Winona, Minn.	10,208	183,000	17.92
Waltham, Mass.	11,711	477,000	40.76
Yonkers, N. Y.	18,892	1,388,000	73.47
Youngstown, Ohio.	15,431	193,406	12.50
York, Pa.	13,940	33,000	2.38
Zanesville, Ohio.	18,120	529,097	29.91

THE ELECTORAL COLLEGE.

The electoral college of 1884, according to the last census, will consist of 401 members, with 201 votes necessary to a choice of President and Vice-President. These votes are distributed among the States as follows:

NEW ENGLAND STATES.

Maine	6	Rhode Island	4
New Hampshire	4	Connecticut	6
Vermont	4		—
Massachusetts	14	Total	38

MIDDLE STATES.

New York	36	Maryland	8
New Jersey	9	West Virginia	6
Pennsylvania	30		—
Delaware	3	Total	92

WESTERN AND NORTHWESTERN STATES.

Ohio	23	Iowa	13
Indiana	15	Missouri	16
Illinois	22	Kansas	9
Michigan	13	Nebraska	5
Wisconsin	11		—
Minnesota	7	Total	134

SOUTHERN AND SOUTHWESTERN STATES.

Virginia	12	Louisiana	8
North Carolina	11	Texas	13
South Carolina	9	Arkansas	7
Georgia	12	Kentucky	13
Alabama	10	Tennessee	12
Mississippi	9		—
Florida	4	Total	120

PACIFIC STATES.

California	8	Colorado	3
Oregon	3		—
Nevada	3	Total	17

Grand Total 401

VOTE OF THE STATE BY TOWNS IN THE PRESIDENTIAL ELECTION NOV. 1880, AND FOR GOVERNOR IN NOV. 1882.

HARTFORD COUNTY.

Towns.	Garfield.	Hancock.	Weaver.	Dow.	Bulkeley, R.	Waller, D.	Tanner, Gr.	Rogers, Pro.
Hartford	4,502	4,727	81	2	3,831	4,684	112	15
Avon	133	110	7		114	103	12	
Berlin	282	264			244	243		4
Bloomfield	140	210	2		120	194		
Bristol	607	625	2	1	574	652	1	24
Burlington	104	159	2		76	157		
Canton	315	222			294	204		
East Granby	100	113			85	98		2
East Hartford	390	410			331	366		
East Windsor	326	259		1	245	239		1
Enfield	734	457	1	4	612	410		
Farmington	342	263	1		318	260		
Glastonbury	436	401	1	8	841	359	4	25
Granby	20	161	3		198	146		
Hartland	90	85	1		93	89		
Manchester	709	455		2	592	455		3
Marlborough	43	55			37	43		
New Britain	1,460	1,326	7	2	1,213	1,425		3
Newington	98	101			92	62		2
Plainville	256	178		1	222	171	1	5
Rocky Hill	127	130	1	1	116	94	4	
Simsbury	213	202	6	8	226	185	1	5
Southington	631	611	16	1	547	558	11	2
South Windsor	212	214	1	2	192	194		
Suffield	465	374	1		403	329	2	1
West Hartford	261	144			213	132		
Wethersfield	266	139	2		236	133		
Windsor	285	291	96	1	227	265	81	1
Windsor Locks	184	272			190	228		
	13,919	12,988	234	34	11,982	12,478	229	93

TOLLAND COUNTY.

Towns.	Garfield.	Hancock.	Weaver.	Dow.	Bulkeley, R.	Waller, D.	Tanner, Gr.	Rogers, Pro.
Tolland	165	134		2	116	127	1	7
Andover	65	61			67	54		1
Bolton	69	73			56	71		
Columbia	83	89		2	82	93		
Coventry	236	242		4	204	216		11
Ellington	169	190	1	2	174	143		4
Hebron	164	119			143	100		
Mansfield	287	181		1	230	136		7
Somers	183	136			158	118		
Stafford	472	476		1	366	368		12
Union	70	92		1	56	63		3
Vernon	835	472	6	6	595	565		21
Willington	173	79	1		143	49		3
	2,968	32,41	7	23	2,390	2,163	1	61

New Haven County.

Towns.	Garfield.	Hancock.	Weaver.	Dow.	Bulkeley, R.	Waller, D.	Tanner, Gr.	Rogers, Pro.
New Haven	5,722	7,917	107	8	4,803	7,871	47	9
Beacon Falls	41	23			64	23		
Bethany	35	118		2	33	113		
Branford	298	423	25	1	210	373	23	
Cheshire	281	232		4	212	195		17
Derby	1,124	1,218		2	1,225	1,117		3
East Haven	412	330	7		93	116	1	7
Guilford	377	288	2	2	310	340	1	
Hamden	311	360	13	3	225	335	1	12
Madison	251	172			194	116		1
Meriden	2,014	1,689	47	10	1,585	1,837	50	19
Middlebury	104	47			70	44		
Milford	374	467	1	2	336	427	3	7
Naugatuck	354	491	8	3	349	434	95	4
North Branford	151	117			111	83		
North Haven	217	150		5	165	131		15
Orange	392	312	1		320	305		
Oxford	108	154			97	137		1
Prospect	85	41			63	36		
Seymour	291	232	1		273	200	2	7
Southbury	173	158			133	158		
Wallingford	427	614		3	333	464		
Waterbury	1,981	2,213		8	1,746	2,045	1	20
Walcott	65	56			65	53		
Woodbridge	117	73			80	45		
	15,714	17,895	212	53	13,095	16,898	221	153

Middlesex County.

Towns.	Garfield.	Hancock.	Weaver.	Dow.	Bulkeley.	Waller.	Tanner.	Rogers.
Middletown	1,139	1,280	45	27	893	1,190	14	53
Haddam	238	319	1		207	281		
Chatham	233	213	1	11	194	206		16
Chester	187	100		1	182	100		
Clinton	200	166		3	174	123		6
Cromwell	199	182	1		182	160		1
Durham	142	129			107	101		
East Haddam	432	263	6	4	322	213	22	3
Essex	291	246		5	256	227		2
Killingworth	76	121			64	107		
Middlefield	126	71		6	109	64		8
Old Saybrook	152	137		1	130	106		1
Portland	376	322	1	1	352	304		3
Saybrook	236	106		3	201	96		2
Westbrook	144	94		6	117	59		5
	4,171	3,719	58	68	3,190	3,334	36	100

Towns.	Garfield.	Hancock.	Weaver.	Dow.	Bulkeley.	Waller.	Tanner.	Rogers.
			NEW LONDON COUNTY.					
New London	1,063	1,103	13	52	771	949	16	71
Norwich	2,260	1,633	25	64	1,691	1,614	19	34
Bozrah	104	77		1	92	69		
Colchester	296	317		17	256	304		17
East Lyme	224	128			184	101		2
Franklin	104	52			78	42		
Griswold	323	195	8	3	214	184	7	2
Groton	602	520	5	6	455	459	19	19
Lebanon	280	149		9	224	120		16
Ledyard	152	170	2		123	148		1
Lisbon	68	81			49	84		1
Lyme	136	121		1	110	102		2
Montville	307	276		10	252	226		6
North Stonington	294	154	3	2	211	219	2	
Old Lyme	121	181		2	88	152		
Preston	267	343		2	211	335		3
Salem	75	74		3	63	62		5
Sprague	95	123	77		85	130		22
Stonington	743	612	11	16	548	575	6	59
Voluntown	170	70	3		140	68	1	
Waterford	312	283		4	179	212		5
	7,936	6,712	147	191	6,164	6,223	93	243
			WINDHAM COUNTY.					
Brooklyn	225	140		5	186	94		7
Ashford	148	160		1	103	138		
Canterbury	153	161			160	113		
Chaplin	98	47			86	36		3
Eastford	124	98			120	84		1
Hampton	123	71			90	62		
Killingly	723	434		2	644	343		5
Plainfield	373	257	1	3	311	225		10
Pomfret	196	95	1		117	78		1
Putnam	515	251	9	1	359	271	5	7
Scotland	90	68		1	84	50		2
Sterling	96	102	2		86	63		2
Thompson	399	151		2	291	111		2
Windham	757	601	2	16	679	501	1	28
Woodstock	406	171		1	334	121	2	3
	4,426	2,810	15	32	3,650	2,290	8	71
			FAIRFIELD COUNTY.					
Bridgeport	2,935	3,391	59		2,352	3,034	30	17
Danbury	1,245	1,167	7		836	987	7	92
Bethel	349	292		3	294	271		3
Brookfield	113	164	1		96	124		
Darien	245	187			165	153		1
Easton	165	153			147	93		
Fairfield	398	414		6	309	311	1	23
Greenwich	794	808	2		656	651	12	
Huntington	296	228			280	230		
Monroe	156	144			151	95		

FAIRFIELD COUNTY—CONTINUED.

New Canaan	319	300		1	278	296		
New Fairfield	60	135			65	106		
Newtown	266	532	1		231	467		1
Norwalk	1,588	1,271	4	2	1,136	936		95
Redding	214	171			160	153		1
Ridgefield	313	210			266	180	1	
Sherman	126	83			122	76		
Stamford	1,086	1,055	12	1	905	892	12	1
Stratford	538	385		13	453	353	4	
Trumbull	172	174	3	1	138	159	1	1
Weston	100	131			91	97		
Westport	287	459			196	351		
Wilton	238	210			177	174		2
	12,003	12,064	82	27	9,513	10,183	71	237

LITCHFIELD COUNTY.

Litchfield	341	381		1	283	341		1
Barkhamsted	144	170	10		134	152		
Bethlehem	95	87			86	82		
Bridgewater	56	132			51	116		
Canaan	154	140		2	78	165		12
Colebrook	102	129	6		78	121	4	
Cornwall	202	188			123	192		
Goshen	117	109	4		90	93		
Harwinton	152	88		3	128	72		6
Kent	180	195			94	184		3
Morris	77	102			55	95		1
New Hartford	313	238	5		266	223		4
New Milford	407	587	2	1	336	525		
North Canaan	127	224	2		124	173	3	
Norfolk	179	116			151	[illegible]		2
Plymouth	296	223		3	199	217		8
Roxbury	107	119			86	124		
Salisbury	311	485	11	6	235	485	1	11
Sharon	254	319			186	269		
Thomaston	399	253	7	3	322	273	4	4
Torrington	451	342	1	1	461	332		3
Warren	103	63		1	51	63		
Washington	188	186			164	172		
Watertown	282	197		1	202	186		2
Winchester	597	555	59	2	493	608	17	7
Woodbury	310	228		3	233	211	7	7
	5,994	5,886	107	27	4,709	5,573	36	68

COUNTIES.

Hartford	13,919	12,988	234	34	11,982	12,478	229	30
New Haven	15,714	17,895	212	53	13,095	16,808	221	153
New London	7,766	6,612	144	192	6,024	6,155	92	243
Fairfield	12,003	12,064	99	27	9,513	10,183	71	237
Windham	4,596	2,880	18	32	3,650	2,290	8	71
Litchfield	5,944	5,886	107	27	4,709	5,573	36	68
Middlesex	4,171	3,719	58	68	3,490	3,234	36	100
Tolland	2,968	2,344	7	23	2,390	2,403	4	63
	67,081	64,118	869	456	54,853	59,014	697	1,033

Total vote for President, November, 1880, 132,862; 39 votes returned as scattering. Garfield's majority, 1,299. Total vote for Governor, November, 1882, 115,698; 40 votes returned as scattering. Waller's plurality, 4,161. Waller's majority, 2,390.

OFFICIAL VOTE FOR CONGRESSMEN THIRD CONGRESSIONAL DISTRICT. NOVEMBER, 1882.

NEW LONDON COUNTY.

TOWNS.	Penrose.	Wait.	Prohibit'n	Gr'nback.
New London	883	904	75	18
Norwich	1,504	1,784	34	19
Bozrah	68	92		
Colchester	314	247		
East Lyme	97	186		
Franklin	37	83		
Griswold	178	219	2	7
Groton	435	471	22	18
Lebanon	119	225	15	
Ledyard	146	124	1	
Lisbon	83	49	1	
Lyme	103	108	6	
Montville	227	256		
North Stonington	212	219		2
Old Lyme	149	91		
Preston	322	215	3	
Salem	52	74		
Sprague	128	87		21
Stonington	561	551	61	6
Voluntown	68	140		2
Waterford	222	173		
Total	5,908	6,298	220	93

WINDHAM COUNTY.

TOWNS.	Penrose.	Wait.	Prohibit'n	Greenb'ck
Brooklyn	93	185	7	
Ashford	139	106		
Canterbury	112	161		
Chaplin	36	88	1	
Eastford	85	116		
Hampton	60	89		
Killingly	375	599	7	
Plainfield	234	299	8	
Pomfret	78	114		
Putnam	267	361	7	5
Scotland	50	85	2	
Sterling	64	86	2	
Thompson	113	287	2	
Windham	493	680	29	
Woodstock	121	328	3	2
Total	2,320	3,584	68	7

RECAPITULATION.

	Penrose.	Wait.	Prohibit'n	Greenb'ck
New London County	5,908	6,298	220	93
Windham "	2,320	3,584	63	7
Total	8,228	9,882	283	100

Wait's plurality, 1,654. Majority, 1,271.

OFFICIAL VOTE FOR SENATORS IN NEW LONDON AND WINDHAM COUNTIES IN 1882 AND 1883.

NINTH SENATORIAL DISTRICT.	1883. Palmer.	Stanton.
Groton	449	458
New London	645	670
North Stonington	153	255
Stonington	501	569
Total	1,748	1,952

Stanton's (Rep.) plurality, 204.

TENTH SENATORIAL DISTRICT.	1882. Barnes.	Ayer.
Ledyard	118	122
Norwich	1,670	1,647
Preston	315	229
Total	2,133	1,998

Barnes (Dem.) plurality, 135.

ELEVENTH SENATORIAL DISTRICT.	1883. Calkins.	Crandall
Bozrah	66	97
Colchester	252	240
East Lyme	159	84
Franklin	44	71
Griswold	135	266
Lebanon	67	241
Lisbon	74	45
Lyme	92	114
Montville	177	234
Old Lyme	93	128
Salem	48	59
Sprague	116	108
Voluntown	102	94
Waterford	167	99
Total	1,592	1,850

Crandall's (Rep.) plurality, 258.

WINDHAM COUNTY DISTRICTS

SIXTEENTH SENATORIAL DISTRICT.	1882. Perkins.	Barrows
Ashford	139	106
Eastford	87	119
Killingly	333	637
Putnam	274	351
Thompson	109	292
Woodstock	122	332
Total	1,064	1,837

Barrows (Rep.) plurality, 773.

SEVENTEENTH DISTRICT.	1882. Marlor.	Boss.
Brooklyn	86	121
Canterbury	152	140
Chaplin	23	66
Hampton	47	74
Plainfield	166	266
Pomfret	123	46
Sterling	45	108
Scotland	49	76
Windham	378	733
Total	1,069	1,630

Boss' (Rep.) plurality, 561.

REPUBLICAN NATIONAL TICKET.

For President—JAMES G. BLAINE, of Maine.
For Vice-President—JOHN A. LOGAN, of Illinois

THE PLATFORM.

The Republicans of the United States, in National Convention assembled, renew their allegiance to the principles upon which they have triumphed in six successive presidential elections, and congratulate the American people on the attainment of so many results in legislation and administration by which the Republican party has, after saving the Union, done so much to render its institutions just, equal and beneficent. The safeguard of liberty, and the embodiment of the best thought and highest purposes of her citizens, the republican party gained its strength by quick, faithful response to the demands of the people for the freedom and equality of all men, for a united nation, assuring the rights of all citizens, for the elevation of labor, for an honest currency, for purity in legislation and integrity and accountability in all departments of the government, and it accepts anew the duty of leading in the work of progress and reform.

We lament the death of President Garfield, whose sound statesmanship, long conspicuous in congress, gave promise of a strong and successful administration, a promise fully realized during the short period of his service as president of the United States. His distinguished success in war and peace have endeared him to the hearts of the American people.

In the administration of President Arthur we recognize a wise, conservative and patriotic policy, under which the country has been blessed with remarkable prosperity; and we believe his eminent services are entitled to and will receive the hearty approval of every citizen.

It is the first duty of a good government to protect the rights and promote the interests of its own people. The largest diversity of industry is most productive to general prosperity and of the comfort and independence of the people. We therefore demand that the imposition of duties on foreign imports shall be made, not for revenue only, but that in raising the requisite revenues for the government such duties shall be so levied as to afford security to our deversified industries and protection to rights and wages to the laborers, to the end that active and intelligent labor, as well as capital, may have its just award and the laboring man his full share in the national prosperity. Against the so-called economical system of the democratic party, which would degrade our labor to the foreign standard, we enter our earnest protest. The democratic party has failed completely to relieve the people of the burden of unnecessary taxation by a wise reduction of the surplus. The republican party pledges itself to correct the inequalities of the tariff and reduce the surplus, not by the vicious and indiscriminate process of horizontal reduction, but by such methods as will relieve the taxpayers without injuring the laborer or great productive interests of the country.

We recognize the importance of sheep husbandry in the United States, the serious depression which it is now experiencing and the danger threatening its future prosperity, and we therefore respect the demands of the representatives of this important agricultural interest for a readjustment of the duty upon foreign wool, in order that such industry shall have full and adequate protection. We have always recommended the best money known to the civilized world, and we urge that an effort be made to uni e all commercial nations in the establishment of an international standard, which shall fix for all the relative value of gold and silver coinage.

The regulation of commerce with foreign nations and between the states is one of the most important prerogatives of the general government, and the republican party distinctly announces its purpose to support such legislation as will fully and efficiently carry out the constitutional power of congress over inter-state commerce. The principle of the public regulation of railway corporations is a wise and salutary one for the protection of all classes of the people, and we favor legislation that shall prevent unjust discrimination and excessive charges for transportation and that shall secure to the people and to the railway alike the fair and equal protection of the laws.

We favor the establishment of a national bureau of labor, the enforcement of the eight-hour law, a wise and judicious system of education by adequate appropriation from the national revenues wherever the same is needed. We believe that everywhere the protection to a citizen of American birth must be secured to citizens by American adoption, and we favor the settlement of national differences by international arbitration. The republican party, having its birth in a hatred of slave labor, and in a desire that all men may be free and equal, is unalterably opposed to placing our workingmen in competition with any form of servile labor, whether at home or abroad. In this spirit we denounce the importation of contract labor, whether from Europe or Asia, as an offense against the spirit of American institutions; and we pledge ourselves to sustain the present law restricting Chinese immigration, and to provide such further legislation as is necessary to carry out its purposes.

The reform of the civil service, specially began under republican administration, should be completed by the further extension of the reformed system already established by law to all the grades of service to which it is applicable. The spirit and purpose of the reform should be observed in all executive appointments, and all laws at variance with the objects of existing reformed legislation should be repealed, to the end that the dangers to free institutions which lurk in the power of official patronage may be wisely and effectively avoided.

The public lands are a heritage of the people of the United States and should be reserved as far as possible for small holdings by actual settlers. We are opposed to the acquisition of large tracts of these lands by corporations or individuals, especially where such holdings are in the hands of non-resident aliens, and we will endeavor to ob'ain such legislation as will tend to correct this evil. We demand of congress the speedy forfeiture of all land grants which have lapsed by reason of non-compliance with acts by corporations in all cases where there has been no attempt in good faith to perform the condition of such grants.

The grateful thanks of the American people are due the republican sailors and soldiers of the late war, and the republican party stands pledged to give suitable pensions for all who were disabled, and for widows and orphans of those who died in the war. The republican party also pledges itself to the repeal of limitation, contained in the arrears act of 1879, so that all invalid soldiers shall share alike and their pensions shall begin with the date of the applications. The republican party favors a policy which shall keep us from entangling alliances with foreign nations, and which shall give the right to expect that foreign nations shall refrain from meddling in American affairs. The policy which seeks peace can trade with all powers, but especially with those of the western hemisphere.

We demand the restoration of our navy to its old-time strength and efficiency, that it may in any sea protect the rights of American citizens and the interests of American commerce, and we call upon congress to remove the burdens under which American shipping has been depressed, so that it may again be true that we have a commerce which leaves no sea unexplored and a navy which takes no law for superior force.

Resolved, That appointments by the President to offices in the territories should be made from the bona fide citizens and residents of the territories wherein they are to serve.

Resolved, That it is the duty of Congress to enact such laws as shall promptly and effectually suppress the system of polygamy within our territory and divorce the political from the ecclesiastical power of the so-called Mormon church and that the law so enacted should be rigidly enforced by the civil authorities, if possible, and by the military if need be.

The people of the United States in their original capacity, constitute a nation, and not a mere confederacy of states. The national government is supreme within the sphere of its national duty, but the states have reserved rights which should be faithfully maintained, each should be guarded with zealous care so that the harmony of our system of government may be preserved and the Union kept inviolate. The perpetuity of our institution rests upon the maintenance of a free ballot, an honest count and a correct return.

We denounce the fraud and violence practiced by the democracy in southern states, by which the will of the voters is defeated, as dangerous to the preservation of free institutions and we solemnly arraign the democratic party as being the guilty recipients of the fruits of such fraud and violence.

We extend to the republicans of the south, regardless of their form of party affiliation our cordial sympathy and pledge them our most earnest efforts to promote the passage of such legislation as will secure to every citizen of whatever race and color the full and complete recognition, possession and exercise of all civil and political rights.

DEMOCRATIC NATIONAL TICKET.

For President—GROVER CLEVELAND, of New York.

For Vice-President—THOMAS A. HENDRICKS, of Indiana.

DEMOCRATIC PLATFORM

ADOPTED BY THE CHICAGO CONVENTION.

The democratic party of the Union, through its representatives in national convention assembled, recognizes that as the nation grows older, new issues are born of time and progress, and old issues perish. But the fundamental principles of the democracy, approved by the united voice of the people, remain, and will ever remain, as the best and only security for the continuance of free government. The preservation of personal rights, the equality of all citizens before the law, the reserved rights of the states and the supremacy of the federal government within the limits of the constitution, will ever form the true basis of our liberties and can never be surrendered without destroying that balance of rights and powers which enables a continent to be developed in peace, and social order to be maintained by means of local self-government. But it is indispensable for the practical application and enforcement of these fundamental principles that the government should not always be controlled by one political party. Frequent change of administration is as necessary as constant recurrence to the popular will. Otherwise abuses grow, and the government, instead of being carried on for the general welfare, becomes an instrumentality for imposing heavy burdens on the many who are governed for the benefit of the few who govern. Public servants thus become arbitrary rulers. This is now the condition of the country; hence, a change is demanded.

The republican party, so far as principle is concerned, is a reminiscence; in practice it is an organization for enriching those who control its machinery. The frauds and jobbery which have been brought to light in every department of the government are sufficient to have called for reform within the republican party; yet those in authority, made reckless by the long possession of power, have succumbed to its corrupting influence, and have placed in nomination a ticket against which the independent portion of the party are in open revolt. Therefore, a change is demanded.

Such a change was alike necessary in 1876, but the will of the people was then defeated by a fraud which can never be forgotten nor condoned. Again, in 1880, the change demanded by the people was defeated by the lavish use of money, contributed by unscrupulous contractors and shameless jobbers who had bargained for unlawful profits or for high office.

The republican party, during its legal, its stolen and its bought tenures of power, has steadily decayed in moral character and political capacity. Its platform promises are now a list of its past failures. It demands the restoration of our navy; it has squandered hundreds of millions to create a navy that does not exist. It calls upon congress to remove the burden under which American shipping has been depressed; it imposes and has continued these burdens. It professes the policy of reserving the public lands for small holdings by actual settlers; it has given away the people's heritage till now a a few railroads and non-resident aliens, individual and corporate, possess a larger area than that of all our farms between the two seas. It professes a preference for free institutions; it organized and tried to legalize a control of state elections by federal troops. It professes a desire to elevate labor; it has subjected American workingmen to the competition of convict and imported contract labor. It professes gratitude to all those who were disabled or died in the war, leaving widows and orphans; it left to a democratic house of representatives the first effort to equalize both bounties and pensions. It professes a pledge to correct the irregularities of our tariff; it created and has continued them. Its own tariff commission confessed the need of more than 20 per cent. reduction; its congress gave a reduction of less than 4 per cent. It professes the protection of American manufactures; it has subjected them to an increasing flood of manufactured goods and a hopeless competition with manufacturing nations, not one of which taxes raw materials. It professes to protect all American industries; it has impoverished many to subsidize a few. It professes the protection of American labor; it has depleted the returns of American agriculture—an industry followed by half our people. It professes the equality of all men before the law; attempting to fix the status of colored citizens, the acts of its congress were overset by the decision of its courts. It "accepts anew the duty of leading in the work of progress and reform;" its caught criminals are permitted to escape through contrived delays or actual connivance in the prosecution. Honeycombed with corruption, outbreaking exposures no longer shock its moral sense. Its honest members, its independent journals, no longer maintain a successful contest for authority in its counsels or a veto upon bad nominations.

That change is necessary, is proved by an existing surplus of more than $100,000,000, which has yearly been collected from a suffering people. Unnecessary taxation is unjust taxation. We denounce the republican party for having failed to relieve the people from crushing war taxes which have paralyzed business, crippled industry and deprived labor of employment and of just reward.

The democracy pledges itself to purify the administration from corruption, to restore economy, to revive respect for law, and to reduce taxation to the lowest limit consistent with due regard to the preservation of the faith of the nation to its creditors and pensioners. Knowing full well, however, that legislation affecting the occupations of the people should be cautious and conservative in method, not in advance of public opinion, but responsive to its demands, the democratic party is pledged to revise the tariff in a spirit of fairness to all interests.

But in making a reduction in taxes it is not proposed to injure any domestic industries but rather to promote their healthy growth. From the formation of this government the taxes collected at the custom house have been the chief source of federal revenue;

such they must continue to be. Moreover many industries have come to rely upon legislation for successful continuance, so that any change of law must be at every step regardful of the labor and capital thus involved. The progress of reform must be subject in the execution to this plain dictate or justice. All taxation shall be limited to the requirements of economical government. The necessary reduction in taxation can and must be effected without depriving American labor of the ability to compete successfully with foreign labor, and without imposing lower rates of duty than will be ample to cover any increased cost of production which may exist in consequence of the higher rate of wages prevailing in this country. Sufficient revenue to pay all the expenses of the federal government economically administered, including pensions, the interest and principal of the public debt, can be got under our present system of taxation from custom house taxes on fewer imported articles, bearing heaviest on articles of luxury, and bearing heavier on articles of necessity. We therefore denounce the abuses of the existing tariff; and, subject to the preceding limitations, we demand that the federal taxation shall be exclusively for public purposes, and shall not exceed the needs of the government economically administered.

The system of direct taxation, known as the "internal revenue," is a war tax, and so long as the law continues the money derived therefrom should be sacredly devoted to the relief of the people from the remaining burdens of the war, and be made a fund to defray the expense of the care and comfort of worthy soldiers disabled in the line of duty in the wars of the republic, and for the payment of such pensions as congress may from time to time grant to such soldiers, a like fund for the sailors having been already provided, and any surplus should be paid into the treasury.

We favor an American continental policy based upon more intimate commercial and political relations with the fifteen sister republics of North, Central and South America, but entangling alliance with none.

We believe in honest money, the gold and silver coinage of the constitution, and a circulating medium convertible into such money without loss.

Asserting the equality of all men before the law, we hold that it is the duty of the government, in its dealings with the people, to mete out equal and exact justice to all citizens,—of whatever nativity, race, color, or persuasion, religious or political.

We believe in a free ballot and a fair count, and we recall to the memory of the people the noble struggle of the democrats in the Forty-fifth and Forty-sixth congresses by which a recent republican opposition was compelled to assent to legislation making everywhere illegal the presence of troops at the polls, as the conclusive proof that a democratic administration will preserve liberty with order.

The selection of federal officers for the territories should be restricted to citizens previously resident therein.

We oppose sumptuary laws which vex the citizen and interfere with individual liberty; we favor honest civil service reforms and the compensation of all United States officers by fixed salaries; the separation of church and state, and the diffusion of free education by common schools, so that every child in the land may be taught the rights and duties of citizenship.

While we favor all legislation which will tend to the equitable distribution of property, to the prevention of monopoly, and to the strict enforcement of individual rights against corporate abuses, we hold that the welfare of society depends upon a scrupulous regard for the rights of property as defined by law.

We believe that labor is best rewarded where it is freest and most enlightened. It should therefore be fostered and cherished. We favor the repeal of all laws restricting the free action of labor and the enactment of laws by which labor organizations may be incorporated, and of all such legislation as will tend to enlighten the people as to the true relation of capital and labor.

We believe that the public land ought, as far as possible, to be kept as homesteads for actual settlers, that all unearned lands heretofore improvidently granted to railroad corporations by the action of the republican party should be restored to the public domain, and that no more grants of land shall be made to corporations, or be allowed to fall into the ownership of alien absentees.

We are opposed to all propositions which upon any pretext would convert the general government into a machine for collecting taxes to be distributed among the states or the citizens thereof.

In re-affirming the declaration of the democratic platform of 1856 that "the liberal principles embodied by Jefferson in the Declaration of Independence and sanctioned in the constitution, which makes ours the land of liberty and the asylum of the oppressed of every nation, have ever been cardinal principles in the democratic faith," we nevertheless do not sanction the importation of foreign labor or the admission of servile races unfitted by habits, training, religion, or kindred for absorption into the great body of our people, or for the citizenship which our laws confer. American civilization demands that against the immigration or importation of Mongolians to these shores our gates be closed.

The democratic party insists that it is the duty of this government to protect with equal fidelity and vigilance the rights of its citizens, native and naturalized, at home and abroad, and to the end that this protection may be assured, United States papers of naturalization issued by courts of competent jurisdiction must be respected by the executive and legislative departments of our own government and by all foreign powers. It is an imperative duty of this government to efficiently protect all the rights of person and property of every American citizen in foreign lands and demand and enforce full reparation for any invasion thereof. An American citizen is only responsible to his own government for any act done in his own country or under her flag, and can only be tried therefor on her own soil and according to her laws, and no power exists in this government to expatriate an American citizen to be tried in any foreign land for any such act. This country has never had a well defined and executed foreign policy save under democratic administration. That policy has ever been in regard to foreign nations, so long as they do not act detrimental to the interests of the country or hurtful to our citizens, to let them alone; that as the result of the policy we recall the acquisition of Louisiana, Florida, California and of the adjacent Mexican territory by purchase alone, and to contrast these grand acquisitions of democratic statesmanship with the purchase of Alaska, the sole fruit of a republican administration of nearly a quarter of a century.

The federal government should care for and improve the Mississippi river and other great waterways of the republic so as to secure for the interior states easy and cheap transportation to tide-water.

Under a long period of democratic rule and policy our merchant marine was fast overtaking and on the point of outstripping that of Great Britain. Under twenty years of republican rule and policy our commerce has been left to British bottoms and almost has the American flag been swept off the high seas. Instead of the republican party's British policy, we demand for the people of the United States an American policy. Under democratic rule and policy, our merchants and sailors flying the stars and stripes in every port successfully searched out a market for the varied products of American industry. Under a quarter of a century of republican rule and policy, despite our manifest advantages over all other nations in high paid labor, favorable climates and teeming soils, despite freedom and trade among all these United States, despite their population by the foremost races of men and an annual immigration of the young, thrifty and adventurous of all nations, despite our freedom from the inherited burdens of life and industry in the old world monarchies, their costly war navies, their vast tax consuming, non-producing standing armies, despite twenty years of peace—that republican rule and policy have managed to surrender to Great Britain along with our commerce the control of the markets of the world.

Instead of the republican party's British policy, we demand in behalf of the American democracy an American policy. Instead of the republican party's discredited scheme and false pretense of friendship for American labor expressed by imposing taxes, we demand in behalf of the democracy freedom for American labor by reducing taxes to the end that these United States may compete with unhindered powers for the primacy among nations in all the arts of peace and fruits of liberty.

With profound regret we have been apprised by the venerable statesman, through whose person was struck that blow at the vital principle of republics (acquiescence in the will of the majority) that he cannot permit us again to place in his hands the leadership of the democratic hosts, for the reason that the achievement of reform in the administration of the federal government is an undertaking now too heavy for his age and failing strength. Rejoicing that his life has been prolonged until the general judgment of our fellow countrymen is united in the wish that that wrong were righted in his person, for the democracy of the United States we offer to him in his withdrawal from public cares not only our respectful sympathy and esteem, but also that best of homage of freemen, the pledge of our devotion to the principles and the cause now inseparable in the history of this republic from the labors and the name of Samuel J. Tilden. With this statement of the hopes, principles and purposes of the democratic party, the great issue of reform and change in administration is submitted to the people in calm confidence that the popular voice will pronounce in favor of new men and new and more favorable conditions for the growth of industry, the extension of trade, the employment and due reward of labor and of capital, and the general welfare of the whole country.

EVANS'

Hudson Cream Ale.

The subscriber, sole agent for Eastern Connecticut for the above Ale, desires to thank his increasing host of patrons for their esteemed favors during the past two years, and again announces that this Ale, which has already achieved such a wide reputation for purity and strength, and which has the unqualified endorsement of the medical faculty for family use and invalids, will continue to maintain its honored rank for those qualities which has given it such an enviable name. He will furnish it to the trade in hogsheads, barrels or half barrels, and also put up in bottles for family use, for which it is especially recommended, being made solely from pure barley and hops, and warranted free from adulterations of every nature.

Especial attention is given to family trade, and all orders by telephone. telegraph or mail, will be promptly attended to by

THOMAS O'BRIEN, GROCER,

Roath Street, Norwich.

WILLIAM BURTON,

Mason and Contractor,

Corner of Fourth and Prospect Sts.,

GREENEVILLE,

WHOLESALE AND RETAIL DEALER IN

Brick, Stone, Lime, Sand, Cement, Hair, Fire Brick, Fire Clay, Beach Sand, Drain Pipe, Marble and Slate Mantles. Manufacturer of Artificial Frear Stone and Plaster Center Pieces, Brackets and Ornaments.

Building Sand, Loam or **Filling,** delivered to all parts of the city at reasonable prices. Also, manufacturer of

Drain and Sewer Pipe,

from best material and warranted of a superior quality.

PRICE LIST.

DRAIN PIPE.

3 inch bore per foot	8 cents.
4 " " " "	10 "
5 " " " "	12 1-2
6 " " "	15 cents.
8 " " "	20
10 " " " "	30
12 " "	35 "
15 " round with flat bottom,	45 "

Y. and T. Branches.

8x8 inch	each,	90 cents.
6x6 "	"	65 "
5x5 "	"	55
4x4 "	"	45
3x3		35

ELBOWS.

3 inch	each,	20 cents.
4 "	"	25 "
5	"	30
6	"	35
8		45

P. S.—Liberal discount from above prices to contractors and large consumers.

M. G. ROARKE'S

Steam Monumental Works

Office, 23 Franklin Street,

NORWICH, CONN.

Marble and Granite Monuments, Headstones,

POSTS AND CURBING

Cut to Order and Shipped to any part of the United States.

A large and varied collection of Designs always on hand and made to order.

☞ Remember that no Granite can be properly polished by hand. Steam power alone can do it. My facilities are such as to enable me to execute work rapidly and therefore CHEAPLY. An examination of my finished work on hand is earnestly solicited.

BOOTS AND SHOES!

We are fully prepared to show the largest and best line of BOOTS and SHOES that was ever shown in this City.

We have a complete assortment of GENT'S HAND SEWED GOODS, in all the styles and shapes that the market affords. Also low and medium price goods to suit all tastes.

Our fine line of Ladies, Misses and Children's low and medium price goods can't be beat. All are invited to examine and will be surprised at the large and varied stock we keep.

With our advantages of buying for three stores WE STILL HOLD THE FORT, AND ARE THE PIONEERS OF LOW PRICES. Call and examine our goods and be convinced.

JAMES F. COSCROVE & CO.,
77 Main Street, Norwich, Conn.

Established 1869.

NOSS'

Ladies' and Gents' Restaurant

No's 52, 54 and 56 Water Street.

MEALS at all hours on the European plan. FRESH LUNCH of all kinds too numerous to mention, 5 and 10 cents. CLAM CHOWDER 15 cents a plate and 25 cents per quart. STONY CREEK OYSTERS received daily and served in any style. BASS NO. 1 BURTON ALE and GUINNESS' LONDON STOUT on draught and bottled for family use. BELINER WEISS BEER, Williamsburgh Limited Brewing Co's LAGER BEER, drawn from the wood. Choicest Wines, Liquors and Segars. Sole Agent for CELERY ROCK and RYE.

J. ADAM NOSS, Proprietor.

HENRY L. PARKER. JOHN F. PARKER.

PARKER BROTHERS,

INSURANCE AGENCY.

Room No. 3 Chelsea Savings Bank Building.

Shetucket Street, Norwich, Conn.

Connected Telephone Exchange.

COMPANIES REPRESENTED.

HARTFORD	HARTFORD, CONN.	Assets,	$4,337,280.00
CONNECTICUT	"	"	1,781,626.00
NORTH BRITISH & MERCANTILE, ENGLAND		"	3,265,874.00
QUEEN	"	"	1,753,207.00
PHOENIX	"	"	1,352,946.00
IMPERIAL	"	"	1,229,323.00
NORTHERN	"	"	1,221,601.00
NORWICH UNION	"	"	1,010,607.00
FIRE ASSOCIATION	PHILADELPHIA	"	4,327,360.00
AMERICAN	"	"	1,712,532.00
UNION	"	"	884,298.00
GERMANIA	NEW YORK	"	2,562,136.00
NEW YORK BOWERY	"	"	912,877.00
BRITISH AMERICA	TORONTO	"	823,578.00
MIDDLESEX MUTUAL	MIDDLETOWN, CONN.	"	428,397.00
NEW LONDON CO. MUTUAL	NORWICH, CONN.		78,200.00

JOHN P. MURPHY,

DEALER IN FINE

Groceries and Provisions,

WATER STREET, NORWICH, CONN.

☞Agent for the National Line of Steamers sailing to and from New York, Queenstown and Liverpool. The steamers of this line include the largest and fastest steamship afloat, the AMERICA, which made the trip across in 6 days and 15 hours.

Greeneville Hotel,

THOMAS CUNNINGHAM, Proprietor.

HAS THE LARGEST AND BEST STOCK OF

Liquors, Ales and Cigars

To be found in the City.

Bass' Ale, Dublin Porter and Frank Jones' Ale always on Draught.

MAIN STREET, between 6th and 7th, - GREENEVILLE.

ANDREW MILLEA,

Merchant Tailor,

188 MAIN STREET,

NORWICH, CONN.

FIRST CLASS GOODS. STYLISH FITS AND LOW PRICES.

SATISFACTION GUARANTEED

J. E. BARBER & CO.

MACHINISTS & ENGINEERS.

ENGINE BUILDERS.

Repairing and General Machine Work.

Mechanical and Patent Office Drawing, Model Making, &c.

No. 7 Ferry Street, Norwich, Conn.

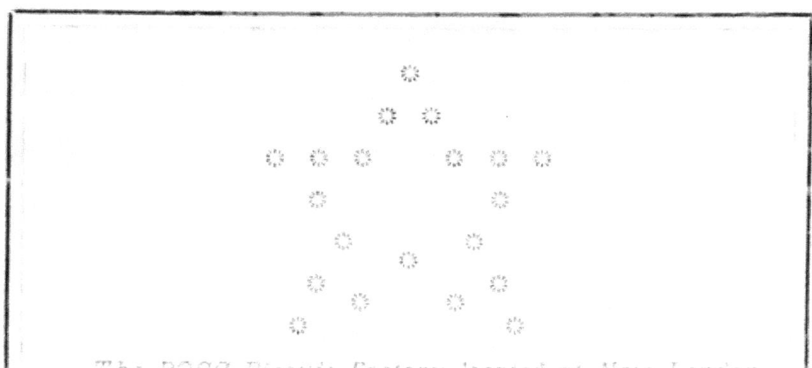

The BOSS Biscuit Factory, located at New London, Conn., is one of the most complete establishments of the kind in America, the capacity of which is equal to that of all others in the state combined.

J. B. SHANNON & CO.,

WHOLESALE AND RETAIL DEALERS IN CHOICE

Foreign and Domestic Liquors,

Wines, &c.

Agents for the Famous Hermitage and Old Crow Distilleries, Bay State and Frank Jones' Ale.

ALSO MANUFACTURER OF FINE BRANDS OF

CIGARS, SODA WATER, GINGER ALE,

At 38 and 40 Water Street, Norwich, Conn.

C. W. BARNES,

—DEALER IN—

Groceries, Provisions, Flour, Teas,

Coffees and Pure Spices, Grain, Feed and Meal.

MAIN STREET, PRESTON, - - - Bridge District.

JAMES MURPHY,

OTRABANDO ROAD, - - NORWICH TOWN,

--DEALER IN--

Groceries and Provisions,

Flour, Teas and Coffees, Boots and Shoes, Dry Goods and Yankee Notions.

ALES, WINES AND LIQUORS.

☞ Goods delivered to all parts of the Town.

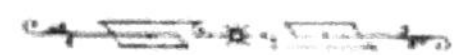

TAXPAYERS OF NORWICH,

AND

POLITICAL HAND BOOK

COMPILED BY

DANIEL LEE.

1884.

PRINTED BY THE DAY COMPANY, NEW LONDON, CONN.

www.ingramcontent.com/pod-product-compliance
Lightning Source LLC
Chambersburg PA
CBHW030539270326
41927CB00008B/1445

* 9 7 8 3 3 3 7 1 3 4 1 0 5 *